For Jimmy La,
a discriminating taster

a SAVOR THE SOUTH *cookbook*

Pie

a SAVOR THE SOUTH *cookbook*

SARA FOSTER

The University of North Carolina Press CHAPEL HILL

Cover photograph by Keia Mastrianni, maker at Milk Glass Pie.

Library of Congress Cataloging-in-Publication Data
Names: Foster, Sara, author.
Title: Pie : a Savor the South cookbook / Sara Foster.
Other titles: Savor the South cookbook.
Description: Chapel Hill : University of North Carolina Press, [2018] |
Series: A savor the South cookbook
Identifiers: LCCN 2018012490 | ISBN 9781469647128 (cloth : alk. paper) |
ISBN 9781469674377 (pbk. : alk. paper) | ISBN 9781469647135 (ebook)
Subjects: LCSH: Pies. | Cooking, American—Southern style. |
LCGFT: Cookbooks.
Classification: LCC TX773 .F715 2018 | DDC 641.86/52—dc23 LC record
available at https://lccn.loc.gov/2018012490

Contents

a SAVOR THE SOUTH *cookbook*

Pie

Introduction

In our home, there were basically two types of pies: my mother and sister's favorite, chess pie, and then my father's and mine, chocolate meringue. Occasionally Aunt June would bring over her specialty, lemon icebox, and Aunt Ann would show up with a caramel pie, just to outdo my mom. I grew up in Tennessee on a farm where the kitchen was the center of our world and something was always cooking on the stove or baking in the oven. Almost every meal ended with a sweet; it could be as simple as a hot biscuit slathered with butter and topped with mashed, sweetened fresh strawberries or a bubbling pie or cobbler coming straight from the oven.

There were many pie makers in our family, mostly women, and no one ever needed a recipe—they just mixed, rolled out pastry, and baked to perfection. With this deep, hands-on experience, it seemed as if anyone in our family circle could throw together a pie at the drop of a hat. These were pie recipes that had been passed down from grandmothers, aunts, and cousins, brought over by a neighbor, or shared at the church picnic. Inspired, from an early age I was in the kitchen every chance I got and developed a natural passion for pies. I also learned at a young age—when my mom got a job at the Fox restaurant in Jackson, Tennessee, and I was introduced to the restaurant's coconut cream pie—that a whole new world of pies was waiting to be discovered.

After attending culinary school in New York in the 1980s, I started working in restaurants throughout the city. I soon realized my preference for grills and skillets and that I would become, professionally, a cook and not a baker. But this did not mean that I would shy away from baking, of course, which I also loved. And here's the benefit of approaching baking as a savory cook: you think more about seasonality, contrasting flavors and textures and seasoning to taste. A peach pie will take less sugar if you have tree-ripened peaches rather than grocery store peaches that were picked before they ripened. Just as a chef does, think about what each season has to offer that's fresh and ripe: strawberries and rhubarb in the spring; peaches, blackberries, cherries, and figs in the summer; sweet potatoes, pumpkins, apples, and pears in the fall; Meyer lemons, Key limes, Cara Cara oranges, and other citrus in the winter. And when you can't find seasonal ingredients, make "anytime pies," with fillings of chocolate, buttermilk, coconut, custard, and nuts.

Even though I chose not to be a pastry chef, I would often be the first to volunteer to make a hundred cherry pies for the catering company I worked with in New York. I made apple pies in our small apartment's oven, which could barely accommodate a pie, just because there were so many varieties of apples at the Union Square Greenmarket. With varieties like Idared, Jonagold, Northern Spy, Jersey Mac, and Cortland, it was hard to resist. There was something satisfying about going through the process of rolling and baking that ended with a sense of accomplishment. Making pies is an art anyone can easily master: it is forgiving of imperfection. You can choose to make it sweet or tart to your liking. Make a pie, learn from your experience, and repeat. Forget all those intimidating stories about "mastering the art of pastry"—this is something easily accomplished with a few attempts at mixing flour, salt, fat, and water. Where do you think the expression "easy as pie" came from?

Pies are found not only in the kitchen but throughout every part of our *southern* culture. If I'm cooking or baking, the music is playing. I have long heard all about pies in the lyrics of our great southern songwriters, particularly in blues. In his 1930s classic "I Want Some of Your Pie," Blind Boy Fuller sings, "You gotta give me some of it, you gotta give me some of it, before you give it all away." From that to Bob Dylan's "Country Pie" to the rapper Domino's "Sweet Potato Pie," read into it what you want. When it comes to song writing, pie has many meanings.

Curly Weaver, a Georgia blues singer, recorded "Fried Pie Blues" in 1934—"If I have any money I will buy me some mmmmmmmmm"—and one of the most popular songs, recorded by more than twenty other artists, is Hank Williams's 1952 "Jambalaya," which includes this line: "Jambalaya and a crawfish pie and filé gumbo. 'Cause tonight I'm gonna see my ma cher amio." And who can forget the chorus line from Johnny Cash's 1970s hit "Pie in the Sky": "There will be pie in the sky, by and by, when I die . . . and it will be alright, it will be alright."

I'll never forget southern literary master Eudora Welty's short story "Kin," in which, on a visit to Mississippi after being away for years, she describes dessert, served at "two-thirty in the afternoon, after an enormous dinner, . . . [a] wonderful black, bitter, moist chocolate pie under mountains of meringue and black bitter coffee." You can almost taste the pie. The scene from the movie adaptation of Kathryn Stockett's 2009 novel *The Help*, for which Octavia Spencer won an Oscar, has a hilarious and telling scene in which the fired maid Minny gives her former employer Hilly her famous chocolate pie. It had us all laughing. In a story Roy Blount Jr. wrote for *Garden and Gun*, the merits of pie come up: "Roy Acuff, the king of country music, preferred to eat his pie first, to make sure he had room for it. Ralph Waldo Emerson believed in starting the day off with pie—ate it regularly for breakfast." But I think this "Song to Pie" that Blount wrote in his book *Save Room for Pie* says it all.

Pie.
Oh my.
Nothing tastes sweet,
Wet, salty, and dry
All at once so well as pie.

Apple and pumpkin and mince and black bottom,
I'll come to your place every day if you've got 'em.
Pie.

Southerners are known to drive off the beaten path for most any kind of food—but especially pie. There are pie shops on the back roads and highways from Virginia to Texas, in trailers, strip malls, service stations, truck stops, and shacks on the side of the road. Pie shops like Charlotte's Eats and Sweets in Keo, Arkansas, are steeped in tradition: Charlotte Bowls makes the best caramel pie with mile-high meringue that you will ever eat.

Here are a few of my other favorite spots for pie. At the Crystal Grill in Greenwood, Mississippi, people wait daily for the coconut cream pie to emerge from the oven. Crook's Corner in Chapel Hill, North Carolina, features Bill Smith's Atlantic Beach Pie, perfectly tart and creamy with a saltine crust. At Ms. Lena's Pie Shop in De Valls Bluff, Arkansas, the fried pies are seasonal. When I went to Ms. Lena's recently, I saw a sign posted: "Fried pies ended for season on Feb. 4th." I asked Ms. Lena what determined fried pie season, and she replied, "Huntin' season." I will definitely travel back to Ms. Lena's. Everyone says her fried pies are the best they have ever eaten—whether apricot, apple, or hunter's pie, made with chocolate, cherries, and marshmallows. At Jessica and Tristan Lehnert's roadside shop, Carolina Cider Company, in Yemassee, South Carolina, you can get peach and blueberry pies in season, and buttermilk and sweet potato pies most anytime of the year.

And new pie shops are popping up, from Brooklyn, New York, where strawberry balsamic pie is a favorite at Four & Twenty Blackbirds Bakery, to Durham, North Carolina, where Scratch bakery offers such specialties as a dark chocolate sea salt tart. These bakeries are only just a few of the new wave of pie shops changing the way we think about and define southern food today, mixing traditional recipes with contemporary flavors.

Speaking of the range from traditional to contemporary pies, the pies we bake and drive all over to find and eat today are not the same as the pies that centuries ago were transported by European colonists across the Atlantic to this land. Historians trace the origin of pie to Egypt and Greece before making its way to Rome. Recipes varied according to the culture and cuisine of the region, but the primary fat used in the pastry by the Egyptians, Greeks, and Romans was olive oil, which made a less than desirable pastry. According to food historian John Ayto, in his book *An A–Z of Food and Drink*, "The idea of enclosing meat inside a sort of pastry made from flour and oil originated in ancient Rome, but it was the northern European use of lard and butter to make a pastry shell that could be rolled out and molded that led to the advent of true pie." The Europeans made pies with small amounts of filling and dense crusts, using little flour and suet, butter, or lard as the fat. They were frequently filled with savory, rather than sweet, fillings. Later pies were baked with many of the berries and fruits that Native Americans introduced to the early settlers. Southerners also developed their own types of pastry using lard, which was plentiful due to the large population of hogs, with many rural folk processing animals raised locally. Only later came Crisco, the choice of my grandmother and many other southerners for making piecrusts. Some used other vegetable shortenings.

The South's real obsession with sweet pies came in the early 1800s, when sugar refineries were established in the United States, sourcing cane sugar from Cuba as well as from plantations sprawling across Georgia and Louisiana. This made sugar readily available and affordable for home cooks, and sweet pies became more widespread.

The growing popularity of sugar is evident in this recipe for molasses pie from *The Williamsburg Art of Cookery*, a collection of recipes known to have been used in Virginia households in the eighteenth and nineteenth centuries, compiled in 1938 by Helen Bullock and still in print today.

Molasses Pie

Four eggs—beat the Whites separate—one Teacupful of brown Sugar, half a Nutmeg, two Tablespoonfuls of Butter; beat them well together: stir in one Teacupful and a half of Molasses, and then add Whites of Eggs. Bake on Pastry (Mrs. Cole's Recipe, ca. 1837. Prov'd Market Square Tavern Kitchen, 1937).

Early southern cooks made pies and tarts from recipes they found in English cookbooks. But they soon learned to develop recipes based on locally sourced ingredients, including sweet potatoes, pecans, peaches, and apples. Sweet potato pie was more than likely introduced by enslaved African Americans, who brought their culture and cooking from traditional African cuisine. Chess pie was popular in the South because cornmeal, vinegar, and eggs were pantry staples.

If you pick up a southern community cookbook, a Junior League recipe collection, or a church cookbook, there will more than likely be no fewer than seven or eight recipes for chess pie, buttermilk pie, and pecan pie. With titles like *Southern Sideboards*, *Come on In*, *House-Party*, and *Jubilee*, these books make it clear that southerners like to entertain and that pie is always on the table.

Some of these recipes, with such names as Company's Comin' Pie, Slices of Sin, Brandy Alexander Pie, Heavenly Pie, Million-Dollar Pie, Grasshopper Pie, and Pink Squirrel Pie, are made with condensed milk, marshmallows, almond liqueur, crème de menthe, and other ready-made ingredients. Although lots of new, more contemporary recipes don't use as many of these ingredients, I do believe there is a time and a place for everything.

Not only southerners are obsessed with pie. Pie is a universal language. You find it in so many cultures around the world, whether it's a tart in England, a galette in France, an empanada in Spain, a crostata in Italy, an Aussie meat pie Down Under, a coulibiac in Russia, or a spanakopita in Greece. Layered with sweet or savory fillings, with regional flavors inspired by international traditions and ingredients, pie appeals to most everyone, as I know from experience: we sell tens of thousands of slices of pie each year at my business, Foster's Market, in Durham. These include Key lime, apple sour cream, mixed berry, chocolate chess, sweet potato, pumpkin, pecan, peanut butter, and many more.

Most of these pies are found in this book, which I am so pleased to add to the *Savor the South* cookbook collection. During some of my recipe-testing time, I was in Lake Placid, New York, a small town of about two thousand people. Once the word got out that I was giving away pies that had been made for this book, I truly felt that I'd become the most popular person in town. I would be walking around the lake, and Rodney, who lives nearby, would give me two thumbs up for the cherry pie I had given him a few days before. At the weekly farmers' market, people I didn't know yet would stop me and tell me how great the blueberry pie was that their neighbors Jan and Jimmy had shared with them at a dinner party. Chrissie, a baker at the local grocery, the Price Chopper, was surprised to find out green tomatoes are what gave the apple crostata that sweet-tart flavor. Peter, my husband, would take hand pies to his golf and liars' poker buddies every week. Soon friends started bringing over wild blueberries and blackberries. I must have made more than a hundred pies throughout that summer, and I shared most every one of them, making for a lot of happy people.

In *Save Room for Pie*, Roy Blount Jr. sums up pie love well: "Every meal, no matter how humble, merits a happy ending— particularly if there's pie." Even when one doesn't want dessert, there is often room for at least a sliver of pie. And as I hope you will find using this book, nothing's more comforting or gives you more satisfaction than putting together that combination of flaky pastry with the perfect filling. Although there are plenty of great places to buy pie locally these days, from farmers' markets to artisan bakeries all over the country, sometimes you just want the joy and pure pleasure of making your own. And you will understand what I mean when your house fills up with that aroma of buttery pastry bubbling with sweet filling. My hope is that this book will help you—like those in my family circle when I was growing up— learn how to throw together a pie at the drop of a hat.

My Tips and Methods

As with anything for which you learn and practice to improve your skills, you need to start with the basics. To you get started, here are mine in a nice handy list.

BASICS

Read the entire recipe before you start.

Understand mise en place. This restaurant technique helps you assemble quickly and effortlessly. It means that you have all your ingredients measured out and ready to use on the counter before you start making the recipe: pans prepared, mixing bowls out, and ingredients peeled, sliced, and grated.

Know how to make a custard. See my tips for making custard on pages 10–11.

Know how to make a meringue. See my tips for making meringue on pages 11–12.

Know how to make a piecrust. See my tips for making piecrust on pages 12–18.

Know how to cream. Blend ingredients—usually butter and sugar—evenly while incorporating air into the mixture to make it fluffy and light. Make sure the butter is at room temperature and not too soft, or it will start to separate. If it is too hard, it will not cream properly.

Know how to fold. Gently mix a fluffy filling or other mixture, taking care not to deflate it, by scooping up from the bottom of the bowl and folding the mixture over gently and slowly.

Know your oven. All ovens are not created equal. Every oven cooks differently, so do not go by cooking time and oven temperature specified in a recipe alone. Do test the oven's temperature with an oven thermometer, and adjust accordingly. Most ovens have hot spots; get to know your oven. Bake on the center rack of the oven unless the recipe specifies otherwise. Always rotate the pan front to back halfway through baking. You will need to adjust your baking if you are using a convection oven: either bake at the same temperature but for a shorter time, usually five to ten minutes less, or reduce the oven temperature by 25° and cook for the same amount of time. Convection ovens have their individual quirks, I have found, but they do make a nice, golden pastry.

Sight, touch, and smell are critical indicators. Use your senses along with the directions for your recipe, as timing in a recipe can never be absolutely exact!

Have the right equipment. Tools that make the job easier include a dough scraper, a handheld pastry blender, tart pans with removable bottoms, a liquid measuring cup, a dry measuring cup, measuring spoons, an oven thermometer, a timer, wire-mesh sifters, pie weights or dry beans, whisks, a rolling pin, a pastry brush, a microplane grater, a juicer, rimmed baking sheets, pie pans and plates, and a non-aluminum saucepan. Some luxury items—not at all required!—include a stand mixer, handheld mixer, food processor, blender, and blowtorch.

Know how to measure. Scoop out a large scoop with the measuring cup, not packing it tightly, and then scrape along the top edge with the back of a knife to level. Know the difference between dry and wet measuring cups (wet measuring cups usually have a spout and handle). Thinking of quarters is a good way to measure thickness—two stacked quarters are about an eighth of an inch thick, and four quarters are about a quarter of an inch thick. Have a six-inch saucer on hand to help with cutting circles for individual or hand pies.

Know how to separate eggs. Crack the egg on the countertop, not on the edge of the bowl, to avoid pushing bacteria into the opened egg. You can pour the egg back and forth between the shell halves, letting the white drop out and keeping the yolk inside the egg shell. Or crack the egg carefully into a small bowl and then scoop out the yolk by cupping the tips of your fingers. Eggs are easier to separate when cold, while egg whites produce more volume when whipped at room temperature.

Know your ingredients and choose the right ones. You know what you like, but I always try to use local, fresh, and seasonal when available, which usually gives best quality.

Think about your overall menu when serving a pie. With a rich steak dinner, perhaps something light, such as Springtime Strawberry Tart (page 104). Bill Smith's Atlantic Beach Pie (page 70) works well with a fish dinner. Apple Sour Cream Slab Pie (page 20) is a nice finish to a roasted chicken dinner. Dark Chocolate Chess Pie (page 48) goes with most everything.

Spices for pie often include these classics: nutmeg, cinnamon, cloves, ginger, allspice, cardamom, and vanilla. But others can also be terrific. Try fresh savory herbs and spices, such as rosemary, mint, thyme, sea salt, black pepper, and cayenne pepper.

Pie toppings may be served atop or alongside the pie to enhance the flavor. Lightly sweetened (and not overly stiff) whipped cream or vanilla ice cream is a classic, but also consider whipped honey blended with fresh ricotta cheese; whipped feta cheese with honey and black pepper; whipped cream swirled with fruit, jam, or chocolate; eggnog; maple syrup; crème fraîche; fruit puree; and fresh berries.

Freezing pie or piecrusts for later. Although your freshly baked pie will likely be eaten by your appreciative family and friends before you can blink, it is easy to plan ahead by freezing whole unbaked or baked pies and piecrusts for up to two months, although one never lasts this long in my house. For a pie or a crust, wrap well, with as little air inside the wrapping as possible, and label with the date. To cook an unbaked pie, place the frozen pie directly in the oven and bake. For a previously baked pie, thaw the pie at room temperature and then warm it in a low oven (about 250°) for fifteen to twenty minutes.

TIPS FOR MAKING CUSTARD

Whisk often. Monitor your heat carefully, and whisk often as the milk heats to bring the milk solids from the bottom of the pan; if these scorch, you will need to start over. The same is true once you add the eggs—keep whisking. The amount of heat and a few seconds can make a big difference for the outcome of your custard.

Do not leave unattended, or your eggs will cook and curdle, and your custard will become grainy.

Use heavy-bottomed, non-aluminum saucepans every time you make a custard. An aluminum pan will turn the custard gray, and the custard will scorch if the bottom of the pan is too thin.

Strain the custard through a mesh strainer if you feel that the eggs may have cooked slightly and the texture is not as smooth as it should be. This is worth a try, though starting the custard over sometimes is necessary!

Separate eggs when they are still cold. Eggs separate more easily when they are just out of the refrigerator.

Whip the egg whites at room temperature. For the best results and most volume, wait until the whites come to room temperature before beating them.

Always use a glass or metal bowl for whipping egg whites. Plastic bowls tend to hold residual oils that can weigh the whites down and prevent them from whipping to stiff peaks.

To whip egg whites, start on medium speed and beat until frothy, then increase to high speed and beat to soft peaks, one to two minutes, and then slowly add the sugar, continuing to beat until stiff, glossy peaks form, usually two to three minutes more (every mixer is different—these times are guidelines, not meant to be exact). You can test the relative stiffness of the peaks by quickly dipping the beaters or a spatula into the whites: the whites are ready if the meringue tips stand straight up when the beater is lifted. At that point also, the meringue should not be sliding around in the bowl. If the egg whites start to break apart or release a clear liquid, you have gone too far: start over and consider it practice!

Do not overbeat! Stop just before you think you are there, since it is better for the meringue to be a little soft than overbeaten. Do not beat meringue past the stiff-peaks stage or it will separate and become grainy.

Cream of tartar, which is acidic, stabilizes meringue so that more volume can be added. A small splash of lemon juice or vinegar, which are also acidic, will do the same.

Prevent weeping and shrinkage by making sure to spread the meringue gently so that it touches the edges of the crust all the way around. It will stick to the crust, which helps prevent "weeping" (the pooling of a film of water between the filling and meringue). Be sure to place the meringue on the pie while the filling is hot. The heat from the pie will begin to cook the bottom of the meringue and prevent a layer of weeping liquid from forming between the filling and meringue.

It will still taste delicious if it weeps. Sometimes I like the way the pie looks when a pretty filling is visible around the edges, so I may not spread my meringue all the way to the edge.

Baking meringue. Always bake a meringue-topped pie in an oven preheated to 350°. Meringue topping on a nine-inch pie will take about eight to ten minutes in a 350° oven — look for golden-brown accents on the tips of the meringue, and be careful to stop baking before the meringue gets too brown. Smaller tarts will take less time, five to seven minutes. But remember, all ovens are different, so don't over bake — just until the tips are golden brown.

Eat on the same day. Meringues are short-lived and meant to be eaten the day they are baked; refrigeration can cause deflation and spongy meringue.

Avoid making meringue on humid days, which can cause meringue to weep.

TIPS FOR MAKING PIECRUST

Keep it cold. Start and keep everything cold — butter, shortening, eggs, and ice water. Many professional bakers even refrigerate the dry mixture. Chop your butter into small pieces and put it in the freezer while gathering your other ingredients. After the pastry is rolled out, chill it again before baking.

Cut in the fat quickly. Cut the butter and shortening into the flour using a handheld pastry blender or a fork (or even your fingers if you can be very fast) until the dough is in pea- to almond-size pieces with a few chunks of butter left visible. If the butter is getting too soft on a hot or humid day, put the entire bowl in the freezer for five minutes, then continue. When the dough is rolled out, you should see streaks of butter in the dough.

Adding the ice water. There's magic in getting to know the balance point where, after you've added the ice water, the dough comes together but is not too wet. Never add the ice water in the same place twice—rather, add it little by little, tossing lightly and spreading it throughout the flour mixture *as you pour.* As you add the ice water, the mixture will change from a dry mix to a pastry dough right before your eyes. Remember: the amount of liquid needed varies depending on the weather and the climate; you might need a little more on a dry day and a little less on a humid day. *Start with about half the amount and add more as needed, one tablespoon at a time, until you reach the right consistency.*

Hands off. As with biscuit dough, the less you handle pie pastry, the better. Once you have added the water, work the mixture as *little* as possible. Use a fork or spatula to get the dough to combine *until it just starts to clump together.* Gently squeeze the dough to see if it holds together, and if it does, do not add any more water. Overworking it will toughen your crust. Once it starts to come together, dump the dough out on a piece of plastic wrap and form it into a flat, round disk. Knowing how much water to add takes experience—you can experiment with this as you bake more pies.

Add a couple of drops of vinegar to your ice water. The acid in the vinegar adds flakiness to the crust.

Rest and refrigerate. Before baking, refrigerate the pie pastry for at least thirty minutes, overnight, or up to three days. This gives the gluten time to relax, helps prevent shrinking, and makes the dough easier to roll. I make several batches at a time, roll the crusts out, cover them in plastic wrap, and place them in the freezer: then anytime I want to make a pie, it's as easy as mixing the filling and pouring it into the already formed pie shell.

Roll and relax. Let the dough sit at room temperature to soften slightly before starting to roll, or rolling will take too much effort and toughen the dough. It shouldn't be too soft or too hard—experience it and see what works. Use as little flour as possible, but *do* sprinkle flour around on both your work surface and your rolling pin to prevent sticking. Always roll from the center of the dough, not going all the way to the edge. Working quickly to keep the dough from getting warm, add more flour as needed. Pick up the dough and rotate and flip to prevent it from sticking to the surface. Dust off any excess flour before putting the dough into the pan. Don't worry about a perfect round or cracked edge; these will be trimmed. You should end up with a round shape twelve to thirteen inches in diameter and about an eighth of an inch thick.

Easy rolling. I often roll the dough between two lightly floured pieces of wax paper or plastic wrap. You can turn the paper a quarter turn every roll for even rolling, and it helps prevent sticking.

Fold and finish. As soon as the dough is rolled out to the right size, fold it in half and place it so that the fold goes across the very center of the pie pan and the rounded edge of the dough drapes over the edge of the pie pan. So, the dough will be a half moon at that point. Then simply unfold the dough so that it covers the entire pie pan, like a full moon. Now press the dough gently into the bottom and up the sides of the pan. The dough will hang over the edges.

For a one-crust pie, trim the edges of the dough (now hanging over the edges of the pan) to about half an inch (unless it is a double-crust pie), fold the overhang under, and crimp or press to make a rim. The crimping can be as simple or fancy as you like on any given occasion—more on this below.

For a double-crust pie, you'll be rolling out two crusts, one for the bottom and one for the top of the pie. Roll out the bottom crust according to the directions above, and then egg wash the rim of the bottom crust. Next, add the filling and place the top crust over the filling. Press gently around the rim so that the top and bottom crusts adhere well, then trim and crimp or press to make your finished edge. Again, the edge can be as simple or fancy as you like on any given occasion—more on this below. Use an egg wash on the rim to create a golden color during the baking. Vents in the top of a double-crust pie are necessary unless you have a lattice top or cutouts in the top. At this point, you may refrigerate again to firm before baking, if you wish. Ensuring that the piecrust is thoroughly chilled before baking helps reduce shrinkage.

For making a tart, drape the dough over the pan and press into the bottom and sides, making sure to draw it up the sides evenly. With a rolling pin, roll over the top of the rim, cutting off any excess dough.

Know how to finish the edges and top of the pie

* *Fluted edge.* Crimp the edge together, pressing the crust between your index finger and thumb with the index finger on your opposite hand. Do this all the way around the rim of the pie.

* *Fork.* Press the edge of the crust against the top rim of the pie plate with the tines of a lightly floured fork. You can get more decorative with this: make a crisscross pattern by turning the fork at a slight angle, continuing around the pie, switching angles each time.

* *Cutouts.* Cut out shapes (circles, leaves, hearts, whatever you like) with very small cookie cutters. Egg wash the flattened edge of the dough and then stick the shapes evenly all around the edges and egg wash again.

* *Lattice top.* It's easiest to do this right on top of your pie, but remember, as always with pastry, the key is keep it cold and work quickly, so read through the following steps before you start. You can make as many strips as you wish, but I like to keep it simple and rustic, without too many strips to weave. I usually use four or five strips *going each way,* but you can use as few as two or three— just make the strips wider.

1. Roll the dough into a twelve-inch round about an eighth of an inch thick and place on a baking sheet in the refrigerator to chill thoroughly.
2. Cut into nine strips, each about one inch wide. A pizza or pastry wheel is a good tool to use for this.
3. Arrange five strips over the top of the pie, in one direction, spacing evenly.
4. Fold every other strip to just past the center.
5. Set a perpendicular strip on top, across the center of the pie. Unfold the folded strips that lie on top of the perpendicular strip.
6. Flip back the alternating strips that were not folded before, and set another perpendicular strip on top, working toward the edge of the pie. Unfold the folded strips again and repeat on the other side with the remaining pieces of pastry.
7. Trim the ends of the strips so that they are even with the bottom crust. Crimp the edges. Glaze the top crust and bake as directed.

Preheat your oven. Always make sure that the oven is fully preheated. Cold dough and hot oven make for a flaky piecrust.

To parbake a piecrust, preheat the oven to 375°. Prick the shell on the bottom all over with a fork. Line the crust with parchment paper or aluminum foil and weigh down with dry beans or pie weights. Place in the lower half of the oven to bake for about ten minutes. Remove from the oven and take out the weights, then place back in the oven and continue to bake on the middle rack for about five minutes longer, if needed, until it no longer looks wet, is opaque and dry looking—and stop *before* it gets any golden color. Watch the crust as it bakes, and if bubbles start to puff up, prick them quickly and lightly with the tip of a little knife or a fork. Remove the crust from the oven and immediately brush it *very, very lightly* with lightly beaten egg whites. This keeps the crust from getting soggy and seals any holes before you add the filling. Have your filling ready, fill the pie while the crust is hot, and place it right back in the oven to continue baking as the recipe directs. (These rules do not apply to double, cookie, or cracker crusts, as you will see in those recipes.)

For a prebaked or blind-baked piecrust, follow the directions above for a parbaked crust, then place it back in the oven on the middle rack and bake just until the crust is *golden brown* all over, about twelve to fifteen minutes.

Store-bought crust. If it works for you, do it—your pie is still homemade (for the most part)!

For extra-flaky crust, give it a turn. Before you roll the dough into a round, give it a turn as you would in Rough Puff Pastry (page 136).

Use up leftover trimmings. Cut small strips, sprinkle them with cinnamon and sugar, and bake for crispy treats that go well with fresh berries or ice cream. Or reroll and make mini tart shells, baked and filled with jam or lemon curd. Or make decorative cutouts for the top or rim of the pie.

TROUBLESHOOTING

Prevent a soggy crust. With the exception of double crusts and cracker or cookie crusts, for a firm result I always parbake the crust (page 16), even for pies that will have more baking time after being filled. You can also help seal the filling off from the crust by brushing the bottom very, very lightly with lightly beaten egg whites as soon as you remove it from the oven. Another option is to sprinkle a thin layer of cookie or bread crumbs on the bottom of the crust before adding the filling.

Prevent breaking the crust or messing up the filling while baking. Place the pie on a rimmed baking sheet before you put it into the oven. Handling the baking sheet is much easier then handling the pie pan when moving it in and out of the oven, and you will be less likely to touch and damage the crust or filling.

Prevent a wavy bottom crust. Prick the bottom crust with a fork to keep it from bubbling up during baking, or use dried beans or pie weights when prebaking.

Prevent a crust from browning too quickly. If the crust or top of the pie is getting too brown before the filling is cooked, cover it lightly with foil while you finish the baking. This may take some dexterity, but foil is very pliable!

LEARNING FROM EXPERIENCE

Make lots of pies. That's how you learn. You'll amaze yourself by how much your hands will teach you through experience.

Fruit and Nut Pies

I get inspired when I go to the farmers' market in the spring, summer, and fall and see rows of strawberries and blueberries and bins of peaches, plums, and apples. I usually let the season determine which of the following fruit pies I will make, because the fruit in season has had time to ripen on the tree or bush; it hasn't been picked and packed while green. Taste the fruit first and let its ripeness determine the amount of sugar you add. In this section, I give you guidelines on how much sugar to add, which depends not only on how ripe the fruit is but also on your own taste. Keep it simple and don't overcomplicate the filling by mixing too many different fruits together. Instead, enhance the flavor of each fruit with vanilla, ginger, bourbon, nutmeg, or black pepper. And if it is the dead of winter and there are no juicy peaches or plump berries, make a delicious nut pie instead—here you'll find chocolate, peanuts, pecans, maple syrup, and much more.

Apple Sour Cream Slab Pie

When fall arrives and the air is brisk, you know it's apple season and time to heat up the oven and start making pies. The best apples are the ones you grow or pick yourself, so try and seek out the heirloom varieties grown in your area. My favorite is the Arkansas Black, known for its tart and crisp flavor. I like a blend of sweet and tart, crisp and tender apples for my idea of the perfect pie, so I add to the tart, crisp Arkansas Black a tender, sweet apple like Macoun or Empire.

MAKES ONE 12 × 8-INCH SLAB PIE / SERVES 8–10

1 recipe Hand Pie Crust (page 142)
6 cups peeled, cored, and thinly sliced tart and sweet apples
    (4–5 apples)
Finely grated zest and juice of 1 lemon
½ cup sour cream
¾ cup granulated sugar, plus more for sprinkling on top
3 tablespoons all-purpose flour
½ teaspoon ground cinnamon
¼ teaspoon freshly grated nutmeg
¼ teaspoon kosher salt
2 tablespoons unsalted butter, cut into small pieces
Egg wash made with 1 egg whisked with 1 tablespoon milk

Remove the dough from the refrigerator and let it sit until it is easy to work, about 10 minutes. Divide the dough in half. On a piece of lightly floured parchment paper, roll each half into a 9 × 14-inch rectangle. Place each sheet, separated by parchment paper or plastic wrap, on a rimmed baking pan and refrigerate.

While the crust is chilling, in a large bowl, slice and toss the apples with the lemon zest and juice. Stir in the sour cream. In a separate small bowl, combine the sugar, flour, cinnamon, nutmeg, and salt and toss to mix. Pour the sugar mixture over the apples and stir to combine.

Remove the pastry from the refrigerator and separate the sheets, leaving one sheet of pastry on the baking pan. Spoon the apple mixture onto the middle of the sheet on the pan, leaving about 1 inch all the way around the outer edge. Top the apple mixture with the butter and brush the pastry edges with the egg wash. Place the other sheet of pastry over the apples so that the edges meet, and cut off any excess dough to make an even rim all the way around. Press the edges with a lightly floured fork to seal. Decorate the top of the pie, if desired, with any leftover trimmings (page 15). Brush the pastry with the egg wash, sprinkle with sugar, and cut 4–5 vents in the top. Refrigerate for about 30 minutes.

Preheat the oven to 400°.

Place the baking pan with the pie on the center rack in the oven to bake for 20 minutes. Reduce the heat to 375° and continue to bake 40–45 minutes more, rotating halfway through, until the crust is golden brown and the filling is bubbling through the vents. Remove from the oven and cool slightly. Serve warm, topped with homemade ice cream or lightly sweetened whipped cream sprinkled with cinnamon sugar.

Blackberry Patch Pie

Blackberries grow along roadsides all over the South. My grand-parents lived on a farm, and in the summer my grandmother would leave a bucket in her car, just in case we ran across a large patch of blackberries on the way home. She would pull the car over and we would get out and pick until we had enough berries for a pie or a batch of jam. She taught me how to select only the ones that would easily fall off the stem into the bucket; these were the plumpest and best for pies.

MAKES ONE 9-INCH PIE / SERVES 8–10

1 recipe Pâte Brisée Piecrust (page 132)
5–6 cups fresh blackberries
3/4–1 cup granulated sugar, depending on the sweetness
   of the berries, plus more for sprinkling on top
1/4 cup cornstarch
Finely grated zest and juice of 1/2 lemon
1/2 teaspoon ground cardamom
1/2 teaspoon ground cinnamon
1/2 teaspoon kosher salt
3 tablespoons unsalted butter, cut into small pieces
Egg wash made with 1 egg whisked with 1 tablespoon milk

Divide the pastry dough in half, and on a lightly floured surface, roll each half into a 12-inch circle about ⅛ inch thick. Place 1 circle into a 9-inch pie plate or pan with the edges draping over and press it into the bottom of the pan. Place the other circle on a rimmed baking sheet refrigerate both crusts for at least 30 minutes.

In a large bowl, combine the blackberries, sugar, cornstarch, lemon zest and juice, cardamom, cinnamon, and salt and stir to mix. Pour the blackberry mixture into the pie shell, scraping out all the juices from the bottom of the bowl. Dot the berries with the butter. Brush the edges of the dough with the egg wash.

Place the other piece of dough centered on top of the pie and use a pair of kitchen shears to trim the edges of both pieces of dough, leaving about ½ inch hanging over the rim. Fold both edges under each other, creating a thick lip around the pie. Use your fingers or a fork to crimp or press the edges of the pie to seal. Cut 4 slits in the top of the pie for air vents. Decorate the top of the pie, if desired, with any leftover trimmings (page 15). Brush the top and edges of the pie with the egg wash and sprinkle generously with sugar (about 1 tablespoon). Refrigerate for about 30 minutes.

Preheat the oven to 400°.

Place the pie on a rimmed baking sheet on the center rack in the oven to bake for 15 minutes. Reduce the heat to 350° and continue baking for 45–50 minutes more, rotating halfway through, until the juices are bubbling around the edges and the crust is golden brown. Remove from the oven and cool at least 2 hours before serving. Serve warm with vanilla bean ice cream.

Blueberry Pie

The variety of blueberries you choose and time of year you make this pie will all be factors in the outcome. The cultivated blueberries in the South are sweet, large, and plump and tend to require less sugar and more thickener than their wild counterparts, which produce a small, tart berry. The blueberry, native to North America, still grows wild in many parts of the country. The cultivated berries we know today were brought to our table by two agricultural pioneers, Elizabeth White, the daughter of a New Jersey farmer, and botanist Fredrick Coville. They crossbred the wild bushes and then harvested and sold what we now know as commercial blueberries in 1916. Cultivated blueberry bushes later made their way south and soon spread throughout the country.

MAKES ONE 9-INCH PIE / SERVES 8–10

1 recipe Everyday Flaky Piecrust (page 130)

5–6 cups fresh blueberries, stems removed

1 cup granulated sugar, plus more for sprinkling on top

2 tablespoons all-purpose flour

2 tablespoons quick-cooking tapioca

Finely grated zest and juice of 1/2 lemon

1 teaspoon freshly grated nutmeg

1/2 teaspoon ground cardamom

1/2 teaspoon kosher salt

2 tablespoons (1/4 stick) unsalted butter, cut into small pieces

Egg wash made with 1 egg whisked with 1 tablespoon milk

Divide the pastry dough in half, and on a lightly floured surface, roll each half into a 12-inch circle about ⅛ inch thick. Place 1 circle into a 9-inch pie plate or pan with the edges draping over and press it into the bottom of the pan. Place the other circle on a rimmed baking sheet refrigerate both crusts for at least 30 minutes.

In a large bowl, combine the blueberries, sugar, flour, tapioca, lemon zest and juice, nutmeg, cardamom, and salt and stir to mix. Pour the blueberry mixture into the pie shell, scraping out all the juices from the bottom of the bowl. Dot the berries with the butter. Brush the edge of the crust with the egg wash.

Place the other piece of dough centered on top of the pie and use a pair of kitchen shears to trim the edges of both pieces of dough, leaving about ½ inch hanging over the rim. Fold both edges under each other, creating a thick lip around the pie. Use your fingers or a fork to crimp or press the edges of the pie to seal. Cut 4 slits in the top of the pie for air vents. Decorate the top of the pie, if desired, with any leftover trimmings (page 15). Brush the top and edges of the pie with the egg wash and sprinkle generously with sugar (about 1 tablespoon). Place the pie in the refrigerator to chill for about 30 minutes.

Preheat the oven to 400°.

Place the pie on a rimmed baking sheet on the center rack in the oven and bake for 15 minutes. Reduce the heat to 350° and continue baking for 45–50 minutes more, rotating halfway through, until the juices are bubbling around the edges and the crust is golden brown. If the crust is getting too brown before the juices are bubbling, cover it loosely with foil. Remove from the oven and cool at least 2 hours before serving. Serve warm topped with vanilla bean ice cream.

Spiked Sour Cherry Pie

When I first moved to North Carolina, we had a sour cherry tree in our yard that produced cherries a few weeks out of the year. If we were lucky enough to pluck them from the tree before the birds did, we would get just enough cherries for a cherry pie or cobbler. Check your farmers' market or your grocer—they may also have sour cherries for a limited time. If so, take advantage and make the most of it by making this delicious double-crust pie, well worth the effort. With just a hint of bourbon, this pie needs nothing more. If you can't find fresh sour cherries, try the frozen ones, which also work well.

MAKES ONE 9-INCH PIE / SERVES 8–10

1 recipe Everyday Flaky Piecrust (page 130)
5 cups stemmed, pitted tart cherries, with their juice
¾ cup granulated sugar, plus more for sprinkling the top
¼ cup cornstarch
Finely grated zest and juice of ½ lemon
2 tablespoons bourbon
½ teaspoon ground cinnamon
¼ teaspoon kosher salt
2 tablespoons (¼ stick) unsalted butter, cut into small pieces
Egg wash made with 1 egg whisked with 1 tablespoon milk

Divide the pastry dough in half, and on a lightly floured surface, roll each half into a 12-inch circle about ⅛ inch thick. Place 1 circle into a 9-inch pie plate or pan with the edges draping over and press it into the bottom of the pan. Place the other circle on a rimmed baking sheet. Chill both crusts in the refrigerator for at least 30 minutes.

In a large bowl, combine the cherries with their juice, sugar, cornstarch, lemon zest and juice, bourbon, cinnamon, and salt and stir to mix until the cherries are coated evenly. Pour the cherry mixture into the pie shell and dot with the butter. Brush the edges of the crust with the egg wash.

With the other dough circle, make a lattice top (page 15) or use a very small cookie cutter and cut out 6–8 shapes in the center of the crust, not going all the way to the edges. Place the round centered on top of the filling; trim the edges of both crusts. Crimp the edges together with your fingers to make a raised rim or press with a fork to make a flat rim. Brush the top and edges with the egg wash and sprinkle generously with sugar (about 1 tablespoon). Place the pie in the refrigerator to chill for about 30 minutes.

Preheat the oven to 400°.

Place the pie on a rimmed baking sheet on the center rack in the oven and bake for 15 minutes. Reduce the heat to 350° and continue baking for 45–50 minutes more, rotating halfway through, until the pastry is golden brown and the filling is bubbling all over. If the top is browning too quickly, cover it loosely with foil. Remove from the oven and cool at least 2 hours before slicing. Serve warm or at room temperature with a big scoop of vanilla ice cream.

Sandhills Peach Pie

The sandhills of North Carolina provide the drainage the peach tree thrives in. Covering a large area a little south of Durham, they are always the first to get peaches in this neck of the woods. Peaches, much like many things we love, have a true following: people swear variously by Alabama peaches, South Carolina peaches, Georgia peaches, Mississippi peaches, and even New Jersey peaches. The point is, the sweetest peaches come from the farmers who leave them the longest on the tree; this is where the peach develops its flavor from the natural sugar in the fruit. And that farmer is the one not shipping the peaches but selling them locally, which is why we all think we have the best peaches.

MAKES ONE 9-INCH PIE / SERVES 8–10

1 recipe Everyday Flaky Piecrust (page 130)
 or Pâte Brisée Piecrust (page 132)
5–6 cups peeled, pitted, and sliced peaches
 (7–8 medium peaches) (see Note)
¾–1 cup granulated sugar, depending on the sweetness
 of the fruit, plus more for sprinkling on top
2 tablespoons cornstarch
2 tablespoons all-purpose flour
Finely grated zest and juice of 1 lemon
½ teaspoon freshly grated nutmeg
½ teaspoon ground cinnamon
½ teaspoon ground ginger
½ teaspoon kosher salt
3 tablespoons unsalted butter, cut into small pieces
Egg wash made with 1 large egg whisked with
 1 tablespoon milk

Divide the pastry dough in half, and on a lightly floured surface, roll each half into a 12-inch circle about ⅛ inch thick. Place 1 circle into a 9-inch pie plate or pan with the edges draping over and press it into the bottom of the pan. Place the other circle on a rimmed baking sheet. Chill both crusts in the refrigerator for at least 30 minutes.

In a large bowl, combine the peaches, sugar, cornstarch, flour, lemon zest and juice, nutmeg, cinnamon, ginger, and salt and stir to mix until the peaches are coated evenly. Pour the peach mixture into the pie shell, scraping all the juices from the bottom of the bowl. Dot the peaches with the butter. Brush the edges of the dough with the egg wash.

Place the other piece of dough centered on top of the pie and use a pair of kitchen shears to trim the edges of both pieces of dough, leaving about ½ inch hanging over the rim. Fold both edges under each other, creating a thick lip around the pie. Use your fingers or a fork to crimp or press the edges of the pie to seal. Cut 4 slits in the top of the pie for air vents. Decorate the top of the pie, if desired, with any leftover trimmings (page 15). Brush the top and edges of the pie with the egg wash and sprinkle generously with sugar (about 1 tablespoon). Place in the refrigerator to chill for about 30 minutes while the oven is heating.

Preheat the oven to 400°.

Place the pie on a rimmed baking sheet on the center rack in the oven and bake for 15 minutes. Reduce the heat to 350° and continue baking for 45–50 minutes more, rotating halfway through, until the juices are bubbling around the edges and the crust is golden brown. If the pie is getting too dark on the top, cover it loosely with foil. Remove from the oven and cool at least 2 hours before serving. Serve warm with a scoop of vanilla bean ice cream.

NOTE * After peeling the peaches, I squeeze the juice from the skins into the bowl with the sliced peaches for extra flavor and liquid to make the pie gooey and juicy.

Straight-Up Rhubarb Pie

Rhubarb works so well in pie that it used to be called the pie plant. The long, slender stalks, known for their tart flavor, pair well with mild, sweeter fruits such as strawberries, peaches, and plums. We're always happy to see rhubarb in the market — it is one of the first signs of spring, and those of us who love rhubarb have long been awaiting its arrival. I love the crunchy texture and sweetness of this pie's crumb topping, which rounds out the tart flavor of the rhubarb.

MAKES ONE 9-INCH PIE / SERVES 8–10

One 9-inch parbaked (pages 16–17) Pâte Brisée Piecrust
(page 132)

FOR THE FILLING
4–5 cups sliced rhubarb (about 1½ pounds),
  cleaned and trimmed
1¼ cups granulated sugar
¼ cup cornstarch
½ teaspoon ground cinnamon
½ teaspoon ground ginger
½ teaspoon kosher salt
Finely grated zest and juice of ½ lemon

FOR THE TOPPING
1 cup all-purpose flour
½ cup light brown sugar
½ cup rolled oats
2 teaspoons ground cinnamon
½ teaspoon ground allspice
½ teaspoon kosher salt
12 tablespoons (1½ sticks) unsalted butter,
  at room temperature

Preheat the oven to 375°. Place the prepared crust on a rimmed baking sheet.

For the filling: In a large bowl, combine the rhubarb, sugar, cornstarch, cinnamon, ginger, and salt and toss to mix. Add the lemon zest and juice and stir to mix. Let the rhubarb mixture sit while you make the topping.

For the topping: In a separate bowl, combine the flour, brown sugar, oats, cinnamon, allspice, and salt and toss to mix. Work the butter into the mixture with the tips of your fingers until it is combined and begins to clump together.

Stir the rhubarb mixture again and pour into the prepared piecrust. Pile the crumb mixture on top of the filling to cover, pressing gently to adhere. Place the pie on on the center rack in the oven and bake for 50–55 minutes, until the top is golden brown and the filling is bubbling around the edges. If the edges or top are browning too quickly, cover the pie loosely with foil. Remove from the oven and cool about 2 hours before slicing. Serve warm or at room temperature with a big scoop of vanilla ice cream.

NOTE ✳ The juice from the pie often makes the crust a little soggy. To minimize this, parbake the crust and brush it with lightly beaten egg whites as soon as you remove it from the oven, before you add the filling. You can also sprinkle the bottom crust with crushed cookie crumbs to absorb some of the liquid.

Sweet and Salty
Peanut and Pepsi Pie

Before the salted caramel trend, it has long been a southern tradition to mix colas and peanuts for that sweet and salty refreshment on a hot summer day. This pie is said to have been inspired by that sweet and salty flavor. If you are fortunate enough to have a peanut roaster and nut butter maker in your area, try different flavored peanut or other nut butters in this pie. For one of the test batches on this recipe, I was out of my traditional crunchy peanut butter and used Big Spoon Roasters' Vanilla Peanut Sorghum Butter. It added so much flavor to the pie that I've used sorghum here, too.

MAKES ONE 9-INCH PIE / SERVES 8–10

One 9-inch parbaked (pages 16–17) Spelt Piecrust (page 140)
    or Pâte Brisée Piecrust (page 132)
4 large eggs, lightly beaten
$\frac{1}{2}$ cup crunchy peanut butter
$\frac{1}{3}$ cup light brown sugar
$\frac{1}{2}$ cup maple syrup or sorghum
$\frac{1}{3}$ cup Pepsi or other cola
4 tablespoons ($\frac{1}{2}$ stick) unsalted butter, melted
1 teaspoon pure vanilla extract
$\frac{1}{2}$ teaspoon kosher salt
$\frac{1}{4}$ teaspoon ground cloves
$1\frac{1}{2}$ cups coarsely chopped salted peanuts

Preheat the oven to 350°. Place the prepared crust on a rimmed baking sheet and set aside.

In a large bowl, cream together the eggs, peanut butter, and brown sugar until smooth. Whisk in the syrup, cola, and butter until well combined. Add the vanilla, salt, and cloves and stir to mix thoroughly. Stir in the peanuts to mix.

Pour the filling into the pie shell and place on the center rack in the oven and bake for 40–45 minutes, rotating halfway through, until the pie is set around the edges and slightly loose in the center. Remove from the oven and cool at least 1 hour before slicing. Serve warm with salted caramel or vanilla ice cream.

Old-Fashioned Pecan Pie

My sister lived in Scott, Arkansas, for a number of years on an old rice plantation that she and her husband restored. A pecan grove on the property produced pecans every year, and each fall my mom and I would schedule a visit around the time we could pick pecans off the ground before the crows, raccoons, possums, deer, and squirrels ate them. We would gather, shell, and freeze the nuts in bags for making pies around the holidays. You still see so many pecan groves driving down the back roads of Arkansan, Georgia, Mississippi, Texas, and Tennessee. These groves have been producing pecans for decades, and I'm sure the grove in Scott is doing the same.

MAKES ONE 9-INCH PIE / SERVES 8–10

One 9-inch parbaked (pages 16–17) Spelt Piecrust (page 140)
   or Pâte Brisée Piecrust (page 132)
1 cup light brown sugar
1 cup dark corn syrup (see Note)
5 large eggs, lightly beaten
3 tablespoons unsalted butter, melted
1 tablespoon pure vanilla extract
½ teaspoon kosher salt
¼ teaspoon ground cloves
2 cups roughly chopped pecans

Preheat the oven to 350°. Place the prepared crust on a rimmed baking sheet and set aside.

In a large bowl, combine the brown sugar, corn syrup, eggs, butter, vanilla, salt, and cloves and stir to mix. Stir in the pecans to distribute evenly.

Pour the filling into the pie shell and place on the center rack in the oven to bake for 40–45 minutes, rotating halfway through, until the pie is set around the edges and slightly loose in the center. Remove from the oven and cool about 1 hour before slicing. Serve warm, topped with vanilla bean ice cream or drizzled with molasses.

NOTE ✳ This pie can be made with syrups other than corn syrup. I have used maple syrup, golden syrup, molasses, and honey.

Chapel Hill Toffee Pecan Pie

This is taking the traditional pecan and chocolate pecan pie to a new level. Chapel Hill Toffee is made with dark chocolate by a mother-and-son team in Chapel Hill, North Carolina. If you cannot find dark chocolate toffee, milk chocolate toffee will be just as good. This is an adaptation of a recipe given to me by my friend Becky Yehia. When I was testing this recipe I considered using a sweetener and thickener other than corn syrup, but what would a southern pecan pie be without Karo syrup? I found this ad from 1917 for Karo, which reads:

> *Save Sugar! But No Need to Do without Sweets—*
> *There's Always Plenty of the Great American Syrup*
> Isn't it a wonderful thing for America that of all the countries in the world, she alone can have this greatest of all grains, Indian corn. Corn is not understood by Europe—by our allies. As patriotic men and women we are asked to change many of our eating habits so that our soldiers and our allies have more of certain kinds of food. But one habit we do not need to change. We have enough of the great American Syrup to spare. One hundred million packages sold last year show that Karo is the country's favorite syrup.

One 9-inch parbaked (pages 16–17) Spelt Piecrust (page 140)
  or Pâte Brisée Piecrust (page 132)
4 large eggs, beaten
1 cup dark corn syrup
1/2 cup granulated sugar
2 tablespoons (1/4 stick) unsalted butter, melted
1 tablespoon pure vanilla extract
1/2 teaspoon kosher salt
1 cup roughly chopped pecans
1 cup roughly chopped dark chocolate toffee

Preheat the oven to 350°. Place the prepared piecrust on a rimmed baking sheet and set aside.

In a large bowl, whisk together the eggs, syrup, sugar, butter, vanilla, and salt. Stir in the pecans and toffee and pour the filling into the pie shell, spreading evenly.

Place on the center rack in the oven to bake for 45–50 minutes, rotating halfway thorough, until the pie is firm around the edges and slightly loose in the center. Remove from the oven and cool at least 1 hour before slicing. Serve warm with vanilla ice cream or lightly sweetened whipped cream.

Maple Walnut Pie

The Noon Mark Diner in Keene Valley, New York, a small town on the road to Lake Placid, is known for its pies. The diner makes about a hundred pies every day—everything from lemon meringue to strawberry rhubarb—but my favorite is the maple walnut. Usually when you pop in the pies are still warm, just out of the oven. It has become a tradition for our houseguests to stop and buy a pie or two (depending on how long they are staying) on their way to Lake Placid. This is my adaptation of Noon Mark Diner's maple walnut pie; it's pretty close and is delicious.

MAKES ONE 9-INCH PIE / SERVES 8–10

One 9-inch parbaked (pages 16–17) Everyday Flaky Piecrust (page 130)

4 large eggs, well beaten

1 cup maple syrup

1 cup granulated sugar

3 tablespoons unsalted butter, melted

$\frac{1}{2}$ teaspoon freshly grated nutmeg

$\frac{1}{2}$ teaspoon kosher salt

$\frac{1}{4}$ teaspoon ground cloves

$\frac{1}{4}$ teaspoon ground cinnamon

$1\frac{1}{4}$ cup roughly chopped walnuts

Preheat the oven to 350°. Place the prepared crust on a rimmed baking sheet and set aside.

In a large bowl, combine the eggs, maple syrup, sugar, butter, nutmeg, salt, cloves, and cinnamon and stir to mix. Stir in the walnuts to distribute evenly.

Pour the filling into the prepared crust and place on the center rack in the oven to bake for 40–45 minutes, rotating halfway through, until the pie is set around the edges and slightly loose in the center. Remove from the oven and cool about 1 hour before slicing. Serve warm with vanilla bean ice cream, lightly sweetened whipped cream, or a pool of eggnog.

Custard and Cream Pies

Custard pies may be the simplest of all pies and likely one of the first types to appear in recipe form. Made of eggs, butter, milk, and sugar and baked in a crust until set, pies like these don't get any easier. Later, custard pies were flavored with vanilla, brown sugar, buttermilk, chocolate, or lemon juice, but they still remained elegantly basic. Because of the amount of sugar these pies contain, they could be kept in a pie chest before the age of refrigeration, and they traveled well. Custard pies in the South are sometimes known as chess pie. Many stories float about concerning the origin of the name "chess pie." Some say this type of pie was originally called chest pie (after the pie chest where the baked pies were stored for a while), and the word was shortened, given a southern dialect, to "chess pie." Others say the name came from the phrase "it's just pie" being slurred into "chess pie." Both theories are entertaining.

As for cream pies, the simple filling consists of cream and milk heated slowly and thickened with egg yolks before being poured into a crust. Sometimes meringue goes on top and then the pie goes into the oven, making those peaks a beautiful golden brown. The pie's creamy filling serves as your base to take on many possible flavors, including caramel, coconut, chocolate, or plain vanilla, topped with most any variety of fresh fruit.

Different thickeners, such as flour, cornstarch, or quick-cooking tapioca, will further define the body and flavor of the custard, as will the proportion of eggs and egg yolks used. I have chosen the thickeners I like for each pie—usually corn starch, which results in a texture that is a little looser than traditional European custard, which holds its perfect shape when cut. As Camille Glenn explains in *The Heritage of Southern Cooking*, "A perfect cream pie filling is never stiff and gummy. It must be soft and should run just a little when cut." In my opinion, this is what we all want to achieve with cream pies. In this book's introduction, you'll find helpful hints on making a foolproof custard (pages 10–11), as well as tips on making meringue (pages 11–12).

The recipes in this chapter are some of my favorites and the ones I grew up on. I encourage you to tweak the flavors to your taste—a little more nutmeg, a dash of cayenne or cracked black pepper, a few berries or cherries dropped in the custard before baking. Some of my best pies result when I run out of one ingredient and choose another instead, such as brown sugar or maple syrup in place of granulated sugar or a few tablespoons of molasses or bourbon in place of vanilla. Let your creativity take over here. Add a little spice and make it your own.

Buttermilk Cardamom Pie

I must get my sweet tooth from my dad because he always had to have a little something sweet after dinner. When there was no dessert around he would make what I now call his favorite "smoothie"; pieces of leftover cornbread in a large glass topped with local buttermilk and molasses were just fine by him. Buttermilk pie was a treat my mom could whip up in no time; with basic ingredients from the pantry, it made a great last-minute dessert. The key to making this pie is to undercook it just a bit to create the delicate, creamy custard. I like to serve it with a pool of blackberry purée or a drizzle of maple syrup. If you are lucky enough to live near a local, small family-run farm such as Maple View Farm in Hillsborough, North Carolina, or Cruze Dairy Farm in Knoxville, Tennessee, where buttermilk is still made in the traditional style, by all means make the effort to try it. Earl Cruze and his family churn all their buttermilk the old-fashioned way, and Earl says, "You make buttermilk the way you raise a family, you care about it. And you taste every batch made." Have all your ingredients at room temperature before starting this recipe, even the buttermilk.

MAKES ONE 9-INCH PIE / SERVES 8–10

One 9-inch parbaked (pages 16–17) Everyday Flaky Piecrust (page 130)
1½ cups granulated sugar
3 tablespoons all-purpose flour
½ teaspoon freshly grated nutmeg
½ teaspoon ground cardamom
¼ teaspoon kosher salt
8 tablespoons (1 stick) unsalted butter
Seeds from 1 vanilla bean
4 large eggs
1¼ cup well-shaken buttermilk (see Note)

Preheat the oven to 350°. Place the prepared piecrust on a rimmed baking sheet and set aside.

In a large bowl, stir the sugar, flour, nutmeg, cardamom, and salt together to mix. Place the butter and vanilla seeds in a small bowl and microwave 30 seconds to 1 minute to melt the butter; stir to blend. Add the butter mixture to the sugar mixture and stir until thoroughly combined. Add the eggs, one at a time, whisking well after each addition. Whisk in the buttermilk until smooth and all ingredients are blended.

Pour the filling into the prepared crust and place on the center rack in the oven to bake for 45–50 minutes, rotating halfway through, until the custard is set around the edges but still slightly soft in the center and not yet puffed. Remove from the oven and cool about 1 hour before serving. Serve warm or at room temperature with fresh berries or a drizzle of maple syrup.

NOTE ✳ To make buttermilk in a pinch: place 1 tablespoon white distilled vinegar or freshly squeezed lemon juice in 1 cup of whole milk and let sit for 5 minutes until it curdles.

Granny Foster's Chess Pie

My grandmother had at least ten handwritten recipes in her recipe book for chess pie, some dating back to 1927. On one of them she wrote in her notes to the side, "For a really rich pie, eliminate the milk and use all egg yolks." I made several versions of the pies in her book, but this one was my favorite, I think it has to do with the method of creaming the ingredients. To make this happen it is important to have all the ingredients at room temperature before you start, even the buttermilk and lemon. Otherwise, the filling will separate and become grainy. There are many variations on this pie, with brown sugar, vinegar, buttermilk, bourbon, chocolate, or orange, but this simple, classic version is my favorite: it reminds me of Sunday lunch at Granny Foster's house.

MAKES ONE 9-INCH PIE / SERVES 8–10

One 9-inch parbaked (pages 16–17) Everyday Flaky Piecrust
  (page 130)
1½ cups granulated sugar
8 tablespoons (1 stick) unsalted butter, at room temperature
4 large eggs, at room temperature
½ cup well-shaken buttermilk, at room temperature
3 tablespoons cornmeal
Finely grated zest and juice of 1 lemon, at room temperature
2 teaspoons pure vanilla extract
½ teaspoon freshly grated nutmeg
¼ teaspoon kosher salt

Preheat the oven to 350°. Place the prepared piecrust on a rimmed baking sheet and set aside.

Beat the sugar and butter together until soft and creamy in the bowl of an electric mixer or a stand mixer filled with a paddle. Add the eggs, one at a time, beating well after each addition. Slowly add the buttermilk, cornmeal, lemon zest and juice, vanilla, nutmeg, and salt and stir to mix.

Pour the mixture into the prepared crust and place on the center rack of the oven to bake for 35 minutes, then move to the top rack, rotate the pan, and continue baking for 10–15 minutes more, until set around the edges but not puffed and slightly loose in the center. Remove from the oven and cool about 1 hour before slicing. Serve warm or at room temperature with lightly sweetened whipped cream and fresh berries.

Say's Coconut Custard Pie

This was my mom's go-to pie when she made pies for special occasions. She loved coconut, and for her there was only one brand, Baker's Angel Flake Sweetened Coconut, the one in the can. In her opinion, the can kept the coconut moist and flaky. I still use this brand of coconut for all the same reasons but can't always find it in the can, so I buy the bagged version, and it makes a great pie, too.

MAKES ONE 9-INCH PIE / SERVES 8–10

One 9-inch parbaked (pages 16–17) Everyday Flaky Piecrust
(page 130)
¾ cup granulated sugar
4 tablespoons (½ stick) unsalted butter, melted
3 large eggs
½ cup heavy cream
Finely grated zest and juice of ½ lemon
1 teaspoon pure vanilla extract
½ teaspoon freshly grated nutmeg
½ teaspoon kosher salt
1 cup sweetened flaked coconut

Preheat the oven to 350°. Place the prepared piecrust on a rimmed baking sheet and set aside.

In a large bowl, combine the sugar and butter and stir to mix. Add the eggs, one at a time, beating well after each addition. Add the cream, lemon zest and juice, vanilla, nutmeg, and salt and stir to blend well.

Stir in the coconut to distribute throughout the filling and pour the mixture into the prepared crust. Place on the center rack of the oven to bake for 40–45 minutes, rotating halfway through, until set around the edges and slightly soft in the center. Remove from the oven and cool about 1 hour before slicing. Serve warm or at room temperature with lightly sweetened whipped cream or crème fraîche.

Dark Chocolate Chess Pie

As a child, I looked forward every year to spending the summer on my grandparents' farm, partly because I got to do things I did not do at home, such as cooking and baking along my grandmother's side. She would always make chess pie for Sunday lunch. I think this tradition started during the Depression because butter, sugar, milk, and eggs were always available on the farm. Still, one reason my grandmother would make this pie for lunch was that she always had the ingredients on hand. I find myself doing the same with this chocolate variation of the pie.

MAKES ONE 9-INCH PIE / SERVES 8–10

One 9-inch parbaked (pages 16–17) Pâte Brisée Piecrust
  (page 132)
2 cups granulated sugar
$\frac{1}{2}$ teaspoon kosher salt
$\frac{3}{4}$ cup unsweetened cocoa powder
2 tablespoons all-purpose flour
3 large eggs
4 tablespoons ($\frac{1}{2}$ stick) unsalted butter, melted
1 cup half-and-half
2 teaspoons pure vanilla extract

Preheat the oven to 350°. Place the prepared piecrust on a rimmed baking sheet and set aside.

In a large bowl, mix together the sugar and salt, and sift in the cocoa powder and flour. Stir until well blended and no lumps remain.

In a separate bowl, whisk together eggs, butter, half-and-half, and vanilla until combined. Add the egg mixture to the sugar mixture and whisk to blend.

Pour the mixture into the prepared piecrust. Place on the center rack in the oven to bake for 45–50 minutes, rotating halfway through, until firm around the edges and slightly loose in the center. Remove from the oven and cool at least 1 hour before slicing. Serve topped with lightly sweetened whipped cream swirled with chocolate or coffee liqueur and fresh raspberries.

Garnet Sweet Potato Pie

My favorite sweet potato varieties are the ones with deep orange flesh—Garnet, Jewel, and Beauregard. They grow well and love the warm southern soil of North Carolina, the number-one sweet potato-producing state in the United States since 1971. For this pie, I prefer Garnets for their moist, orange flesh and earthy flavor. If you like a sweeter pie, choose Beauregard or the varieties that grow near or in your region that you know and like best. Baking the sweet potatoes intensifies their natural sugars and gives the pie a rich, caramelized flavor. Make sure the sweet potatoes bake until completely soft to mash and blend well with the other ingredients.

MAKES ONE 9-INCH PIE / SERVES 8–10

One 9-inch parbaked (pages 16–17) Spelt Piecrust (page 140)
  or Pâte Brisée Piecrust (page 132)
2 cups sweet potato purée (see Note)
½ cup coconut milk, well shaken
3 large eggs, lightly beaten
½ cup light brown sugar
⅓ cup maple syrup
3 tablespoons unsalted butter, melted
2 teaspoons pure vanilla extract
1 tablespoon finely grated orange zest
1 teaspoon ground ginger
½ teaspoon ground cloves
½ teaspoon freshly grated nutmeg
½ teaspoon kosher salt
¼ teaspoon freshly ground black pepper
1 cup gingersnap crumbs (see Note)

Preheat the oven to 350°. Place the prepared crust on a rimmed baking sheet and set aside.

In a medium bowl, whisk together the sweet potato purée, coconut milk, eggs, brown sugar, syrup, butter, and vanilla until well blended. Stir in the orange zest. In a separate small bowl, combine the ginger, cloves, nutmeg, salt, and pepper and stir to combine. Whisk the spices into the sweet potato mixture until smooth and well blended.

Spread the gingersnap crumbs evenly over the bottom of the prepared crust, and pour the sweet potato mixture over the gingersnaps. Place on the center rack of the oven and bake for 40–45 minutes, rotating halfway through, until set around the edges and still a little loose in the center. Remove from the oven and cool about 1 hour before slicing. Serve warm or at room temperature with a dollop of lightly sweetened whipped cream or a pool of eggnog and a drizzle of molasses or maple syrup.

NOTES ❋ To make the sweet potato purée, preheat the oven to 400°. Wash 2–3 medium-size sweet potatoes and wrap in foil. Place in the oven to bake for 50–55 minutes, until soft to the touch. Unwrap and cool enough to handle. While still warm, slit the skins with a knife and slip the flesh from the skins. Place the flesh in the bowl of a food processer fitted with the metal blade and purée until completely smooth.

To make the gingersnap crumbs, place 5–8 gingersnaps (depending on their size) in the bowl of a food processor fitted with a metal blade, breaking them into pieces as you add them. Pulse 5–8 times, then with the motor running, 30 seconds to 1 minute, purée into crumbs.

Banana Cream Pie

This was by far the most popular of all the pies I gave away when I was testing recipes for this book: everyone in my neighborhood wanted to try the Banana Cream Pie. I understand now why it was named the armed forces' favorite dessert in 1951—it still seems to be a favorite for many. Making the crust with vanilla wafers in place of graham crackers gives it that banana-pudding-in-a-pie taste.

MAKES ONE 9-INCH PIE / SERVES 8–10

One 9-inch prebaked Graham Cracker Crust or vanilla wafer
  variation (page 145)

FOR THE FILLING
2½ cups milk
1 vanilla bean, split in half, seeds scraped
¼ teaspoon kosher salt
¾ cup granulated sugar
¼ cup cornstarch
4 large egg yolks
4 tablespoons (½ stick) unsalted butter
2 ripe bananas

FOR THE TOPPING
1 cup heavy cream
¼ cup granulated sugar

For the filling: Place the milk in a heavy-bottomed, non-aluminum saucepan over medium heat. Add the vanilla bean, seeds, and salt and whisk to mix. To scald the milk, bring it to just under a boil, whisking often: the milk will start to steam and bubble around the edges. Remove from the heat and discard the vanilla bean.

In a large bowl, mix together the sugar and cornstarch. Add the egg yolks and whisk until combined. Slowly add about 1 cup of the warm milk mixture, whisking constantly, to temper the eggs. Whisk the egg mixture back into the remaining milk mixture in the saucepan and place back over medium-low heat. Continue to cook, whisking constantly, until the mixture thickens, 3–4 minutes more. You want to see a few bubbles begin to rise slowly from the bottom of the pan. Do not allow the mixture to come to a full boil or cook too long—you will overcook the eggs. The mixture is thick enough when the whisk leaves tracks as you stir. Immediately transfer the custard to a bowl to stop the cooking process. Add the butter and whisk until melted. Place a layer of plastic wrap directly on the custard and set aside to cool slightly.

Slice the bananas and place them on the bottom of the prepared crust. Once the filling has cooled to room temperature, spread evenly over the bananas and refrigerate until firm, at least 2 hours or overnight.

For the topping: When ready to serve, place the heavy cream in a medium bowl and beat with an electric mixer on high speed until soft peaks form. Add the sugar and continue to beat just to combine. Remove the pie from the refrigerator. Top with the whipped cream, slice, and serve cold or refrigerate until ready to serve.

Burnt Caramel Pie with Swiss Meringue

My version of this old-time pie is adapted from a recipe by Mrs. Charles B. Kay in The Somerville Cookbook *from Somerville, Tennessee. The original recipe calls for oleo and sweet milk, and has these directions: "Into a saucepan pour 1½ cups of sugar, ½ cup flour, salt, egg yolks beaten with the milk. Into a skillet put 1 cup sugar to caramelize. Turn heat on both at the same time. When sugar has caramelized the other mixture will have started boiling." Reading these instructions makes you realize that the generation who put together these community cookbooks assumed most everyone knew how to cook.*

MAKES ONE 9-INCH PIE / SERVES 8–10

One 9-inch prebaked (page 17) Everyday Flaky Piecrust (page 130) or Pâte Brisée Piecrust (page 132)

FOR THE FILLING
2 cups granulated sugar, divided
5 tablespoons cornstarch
¼ teaspoon kosher salt
2 cups milk
4 egg large yolks
1 teaspoon pure vanilla extract
4 tablespoons (½ stick) unsalted butter

FOR THE TOPPING
4 large egg whites
¾ cup granulated sugar
¼ teaspoon kosher salt

Preheat the oven to 350°. Place the prepared crust on a rimmed baking sheet and set aside.

For the filling: Place 1 cup of the sugar in a heavy-bottomed skillet set on the stovetop, but do not turn on the heat.

Place the remaining sugar, cornstarch, and salt in a heavy-bottomed, non-aluminum saucepan and whisk to mix. Place over medium heat and slowly whisk in the milk until smooth. Stir constantly until the mixture is steaming around the edges and the sugar has dissolved; do not boil. Remove from the heat.

Beat the egg yolks with the vanilla in a medium bowl. Whisk about 1 cup of the warm milk mixture into the yolks to temper them. Slowly whisk the egg mixture back into the milk mixture over medium-low heat. Continue to whisk constantly until the mixture thickens and coats the back of a spoon, 3–4 minutes more. Do not let the mixture come to a full boil. The mixture is thick enough when the whisk leaves tracks as you stir and just begins to bubble up from the bottom of the pan. Remove from the heat and transfer to a large bowl. Set the bowl aside while you make the caramel.

To caramelize the sugar, place the skillet over medium heat, shaking the pan until the sugar starts to brown. Continue shaking until the sugar turns deep amber and starts to smoke slightly, 3–4 minutes more. Immediately turn off the heat and wait for the caramel to stop bubbling.

Carefully and slowly, pour the caramel into the custard, whisking constantly, until all the caramel is incorporated into the custard. Stir in the butter until it has melted, and set aside while you make the meringue.

For the topping: Place the egg whites, sugar, and salt in a large heatproof bowl over a pot of simmering water, making sure that the bottom of the bowl does not touch the water. Whisk constantly until the sugar dissolves and the whites are hot,

3–5 minutes. You will know that the whites are hot when you see a whiff of steam come from the bowl as you whisk.

Remove from the heat and beat with an electric mixer, on medium speed, until soft peaks form, 1–2 minutes. Increase the speed to high and continue to beat until stiff, glossy peaks form, 2–3 minutes more. You will know they are ready if the tips of the meringue curl over when the beater is lifted and the meringue does not slide around in the bowl. (If the egg whites start to break apart or release a clear liquid, you have gone too far; start over and consider it practice.)

Pour the filling into the prepared crust and dollop the meringue on top, spreading evenly with a spatula to cover the caramel mixture and going to the edges of the crust. Dip the back of the spatula into the meringue and pull it up to create peaks. Place on the center rack in the oven to bake for 8–10 minutes, until tips of the meringue are golden brown. Remove from the oven and cool about 3 hours before slicing.

Over the Moon Pie with the Marshmallow Meringue

The Moon Pie, a classic southern treat, is often paired with an RC Cola and is still made by the bakery in Chattanooga, Tennessee, that started it all in 1917. Earl Mitchell, a traveling salesman for the bakery, asked a Kentucky coal miner what snack sounded good to him, and his reply was "something with graham crackers and marshmallows and as big as the moon." This pie was inspired by that great treat many of us grew up with and still love today. A graham cracker crust filled with chocolate and caramel topped with marshmallow meringue takes it over the top (or the moon). This pie is also delicious topped with lightly sweetened whipped cream if you choose not to make the meringue.

MAKES ONE 9-INCH PIE / SERVES 8–10

One 9-inch prebaked Graham Cracker Crust (page 145)

FOR THE CARAMEL LAYER
½ cup heavy cream
1 vanilla bean, split in half, seeds scraped
1 cup granulated sugar
¼ cup water
2 tablespoons light corn syrup
¼ teaspoon kosher salt
4 tablespoons (½ stick) unsalted butter,
 cut into small pieces

FOR THE CHOCOLATE LAYER
¾ cup granulated sugar
½ teaspoon kosher salt
¼ cup unsweetened cocoa powder
3 tablespoons cornstarch
2½ cups milk

4 large egg yolks

4 ounces (about 1 cup) bittersweet chocolate, finely chopped

2 tablespoons (¼ stick) unsalted butter, cut into small pieces

2 teaspoons pure vanilla extract

3 large egg whites

½ teaspoon cream of tartar

Pinch of kosher salt

⅓ cup granulated sugar

1 cup marshmallow cream

For the caramel layer: Pour the cream into a heavy-bottomed, non-aluminum saucepan; add the vanilla bean and seeds. Place over medium heat and bring to just under a boil, stirring occasionally just to scald the cream, until it is steaming around the edges.

In a separate deep, heavy-bottomed saucepan, combine the sugar, water, corn syrup, and salt. Stir to mix and bring to a boil over medium heat. Continue to boil, without stirring, swirling the pan occasionally, until the mixture is amber colored, 5–8 minutes.

Remove the caramel from the heat. Slowly add the cream, pouring it to the side of the pan; it will boil rapidly. When it stops boiling, whisk until smooth and allow to cool for about 10 minutes. Whisk in the butter until melted and smooth. Whisk the caramel periodically as it cools. Once it has cooled to room temperature, spread the caramel in the bottom of the prepared crust and refrigerate the crust to chill and firm.

For the chocolate layer: Meanwhile, combine the sugar and salt in a heavy-bottomed, non-aluminum saucepan. Sift in the cocoa and cornstarch and stir to mix. Place over medium heat and slowly whisk in the milk until smooth. Stir constantly until the mixture is steaming around the edges and the sugar has dissolved; do not boil. Remove from the heat.

Beat the egg yolks in a bowl and whisk in about 1 cup of the warm milk mixture to temper the yolks. Pour the egg mixture back into the saucepan and whisk to combine. Place back over medium-low heat and cook, whisking constantly, just until bubbles start to come up from the bottom of the pan, 3–4 minutes more. Do not let the mixture come to a full boil. The mixture is thick enough when the whisk leaves tracks as you stir and reaches the consistency of pudding.

Remove from the heat and whisk in the chocolate, butter, and vanilla until the butter and chocolate melt. Cool to room temperature, whisking occasionally. Pour the chocolate filling over the caramel filling, spreading evenly. Cover with plastic wrap and refrigerate until set and firm, at least 4 hours or overnight.

For the topping: When ready to serve, preheat the oven to 350°.

Remove the pie from the refrigerator and place it on a rimmed baking sheet. Beat the egg whites in a large metal or glass bowl with an electric mixer on medium speed until foamy, about 30 seconds. Add the cream of tartar and salt and beat on high, 1–2 minutes, until soft peaks form. Slowly add the sugar, about 2 tablespoons at a time, and continue to beat until glossy peaks form, 2–3 minutes more. You will know they are ready if the tips of the meringue stand straight up when the beater is lifted and the meringue does not slide around in the bowl. Beat about ⅓ of the marshmallow cream into the egg white mixture, just to blend well. Repeat with the remaining marshmallow cream, ⅓ at a time, beating until smooth, about 30 seconds longer.

Dollop the meringue over the top of the pie, spreading evenly to cover the chocolate mixture and going to the edges of the crust. Place the pie on the center rack in the oven to bake about 8–10 minutes, until the tips of the meringue are golden brown. Remove from the oven and cool before slicing. The filling should still be cold and the meringue at room temperature. Slice and serve.

Chocolate Meringue Pie

My sister and I would race to our grandparents' house every Sunday after church to have lunch. There was always pie, and quite often, because it was my favorite, we would have chocolate meringue. I made a small adjustment to my grandmother's recipe with the addition of chocolate chips to give the pie a deep chocolate flavor. I have found that meringue does not do well after refrigerated: this pie is best eaten the day you make it. If I have some leftover for the next day, I scrape off the meringue and serve it topped with a dollop of lightly sweetened whipped cream.

MAKES ONE 9-INCH PIE / SERVES 8–10

One 9-inch prebaked (page 17) Pâte Brisée Piecrust (page 132)

FOR THE FILLING

1 cup granulated sugar

½ teaspoon kosher salt

¼ cup unsweetened cocoa powder

¼ cup cornstarch

2½ cups milk

4 large egg yolks

4 ounces (about 1 cup) semisweet chocolate chips

3 tablespoons unsalted butter, cut into small pieces

2 teaspoons pure vanilla extract

FOR THE TOPPING

4 large egg whites

½ teaspoon cream of tartar

Pinch of kosher salt

⅓ cup granulated sugar

Preheat the oven to 350°. Place the prepared crust on a rimmed baking sheet and set aside.

For the filling: Combine the sugar and salt in a heavy-bottomed, non-aluminum saucepan, sift in the cocoa and cornstarch and stir to mix. Place over medium heat and slowly whisk in the milk until smooth. Stir constantly until the mixture is steaming around the edges and the sugar has dissolved; do not boil. Remove from the heat.

Beat the egg yolks in a bowl and whisk in about 1 cup of the warm milk to temper the yolks. Pour the egg mixture back into the saucepan and whisk to combine. Place back over medium-low heat and cook, whisking constantly, just until bubbles start to come up from the bottom of the pan, 3–4 minutes more. Do not let the mixture come to a full boil. The mixture is thick enough when the whisk leaves tracks as you stir.

Remove from the heat and whisk in the chocolate chips, butter, and vanilla until the chocolate and butter melt. Pour the filling into the prepared piecrust.

For the topping: Beat the egg whites in a large metal or glass bowl with and an electric mixer, on medium speed until foamy, about 30 seconds. Add the cream of tartar and salt and increase the speed to high, continue beating for 1–2 minutes until soft peaks form. Slowly add the sugar, about 2 tablespoons at a time, and continue to beat until stiff glossy peaks form, 2–3 minutes more. You will know they are ready if the tips of the meringue stand straight up when the beater is lifted and the meringue does not slide around in the bowl. (If the egg whites start to break apart or release a clear liquid, you have gone too far; start over and consider it practice.)

Dollop the meringue over the top of the pie, spreading evenly to cover the chocolate mixture while it is still warm and going to the edges of the crust. Place on the center rack in the oven to bake for about 8–10 minutes, until the tips of the meringue are golden brown. Remove from the oven and cool about 3 hours before slicing.

Coconut Cream Meringue Pie

Paying off a debt can sometimes be a good thing. Thanks to a Cuban businessman who paid his debt to the Philadelphia flour miller Franklin Baker with a shipload of coconuts, shredded coconut is widely available. Soon after Baker set up his factory for shredding and drying coconut around 1895, coconut cream pie started popping up everywhere. I sometimes make this pie as an icebox pie, using the same recipe for the filling and spreading it in the Black Bottom Crust (page 146), topped with lightly sweetened whipped cream and toasted coconut flakes.

MAKES ONE 9-INCH PIE / SERVES 8–10

One 9-inch prebaked (page 17) Everyday Flaky Piecrust (page 130)

FOR THE FILLING

¾ cup granulated sugar

¼ cup cornstarch

½ teaspoon kosher salt

2 cups milk

4 large egg yolks

2 cups sweetened flaked coconut, plus more for sprinkling on top

6 tablespoons (¾ stick) unsalted butter, cut into small pieces

2 teaspoons pure vanilla extract

FOR THE TOPPING

4 large egg whites

½ teaspoon cream tartar

Pinch of kosher salt

⅓ cup granulated sugar

1 tablespoon flaked sweetened coconut for garnish

Preheat the oven to 350°. Place the prepared crust on a rimmed baking sheet and set aside.

For the filling: Mix together the sugar, cornstarch, and salt in a large heavy-bottomed, non-aluminum saucepan and stir to mix. Place over medium heat and slowly whisk in the milk until smooth. Stir constantly until the mixture is steaming around the edges and the sugar has dissolved; do not boil. Remove from the heat.

Whisk together the egg yolks in a medium bowl. Slowly whisk in about 1 cup of the warm milk mixture to temper the eggs. Whisk the egg mixture back into the milk mixture in the saucepan and place over medium-low heat. Continue to cook, whisking constantly, until the mixture thickens and begins to slightly bubble up from the bottom of the pan, 3–4 minutes. Do not let the mixture come to a full boil. The mixture is thick enough when the whisk leaves tracks as you stir and reaches the consistency of pudding.

Remove the mixture from the heat and stir in the coconut, butter, and vanilla to melt the butter and combine. Spread the filling evenly in the prepared piecrust and set aside.

For the topping: Beat the egg whites in a large metal or glass bowl with an electric mixer on medium speed until foamy, about 30 seconds. Add the cream of tartar and salt and beat on high, 1–2 minutes, until soft peaks form. Slowly add the sugar, about 2 tablespoons at a time, and continue to beat until stiff, glossy peaks form, 2–3 minutes more. You will know they are ready if the tips of the meringue stand straight up when the beater is lifted and the meringue does not slide around in the bowl. (If the egg whites start to break apart or release a clear liquid, you have gone too far; start over and consider it practice.)

Dollop the meringue on top of the pie, spreading evenly with a spatula to cover the coconut mixture and going to the edges of the crust while the filling is still warm. Dip the back of the spatula into the meringue and pull it up to create peaks. Sprinkle coconut on top of the meringue. Place the pie on the center rack in the oven to bake for about 8–10 minutes, until the tips of the meringue are golden brown.

Remove from the oven and cool about 3 hours before slicing. This pie is best eaten the day it is made; meringues do not keep well in the refrigerator.

Phoebe's Sweet Potato Cream Pie

At Scratch bakery in Durham, North Carolina, Phoebe Lawless has been turning out pies since 2008. Starting as a one-woman operation at the Durham Farmers' Market, she now has the bakery and a restaurant, where she whips up everything from Shaker lemon pie to sea salt chocolate crostatas on the sweet side. And on the savory side (my favorite), she makes pigs in a blanket, squash and apple crostatas, turnip and sausage empanadas, and many more flavorful pies, all driven by the seasons. If you're looking for a good gluten-free crust for other pies, the crust in this recipe is a great option.

MAKES ONE 9-INCH PIE / SERVES 8–10

FOR THE CRUST
1½ cup rolled oats
¼ cup sesame seeds
2 tablespoons granulated sugar
½ teaspoon kosher salt
6 tablespoons (¾ stick) unsalted butter, melted

FOR THE CARAMEL LAYER
½ cup heavy cream
1 cup granulated sugar
¼ cup water
¼ teaspoon kosher salt

FOR THE FILLING
1¼ cups milk
½ vanilla bean, seeds scraped
¾ cup granulated sugar
¼ cup cornstarch
½ teaspoon ground cinnamon
¼ teaspoon ground ginger
¼ teaspoon freshly ground black pepper
¼ teaspoon kosher salt

2 large eggs
2 large egg yolks
1 cup sweet potato purée (see Note)
4 tablespoons (½ stick) unsalted butter

FOR THE TOPPING
1 cup heavy cream
¼ cup granulated sugar

For the crust: Preheat the oven to 350°.

Combine the oats, sesame seeds, sugar, and salt in the bowl of a food processor and pulse to crush the oats. (Do not pulse to a fine dust; the crumbs will have small pieces remaining.) Add the melted butter and pulse until the dry ingredients are moistened.

Press the mixture evenly on the bottom and up the sides of the pan to form the crust. Freeze or refrigerate for 30 minutes until firm.

Place the pie pan on a rimmed baking sheet on the center rack in the oven to bake just until golden brown, 15–20 minutes. Remove from the oven and set aside to cool.

For the caramel layer: Pour the cream into a heavy-bottomed, non-aluminum saucepan over medium heat and bring to just under a boil, stirring occasionally, to warm the cream. Remove from the heat and set aside.

In a separate deep, heavy saucepan-bottomed, combine the sugar, water, and salt. Stir to mix and bring to a boil over medium heat. Continue to boil without stirring, swirling the pan occasionally, until the mixture is amber colored, 5–8 minutes. Remove the caramel from the heat. Slowly add the cream, pouring it to the side of the pan; it will boil rapidly. When it stops boiling, whisk until smooth and allow to cool. Whisk the caramel periodically as it continues to cool. Once cooled to room temperature, spread in the bottom of the prepared crust and refrigerate until firm.

For the custard layer: Place the milk in a heavy-bottomed, non-aluminum saucepan over medium heat. Add the vanilla bean and seeds and whisk to mix. To scald the milk, bring to just under a boil, whisking often. The milk will start to bubble around the edges and steam. Remove from the heat and discard the vanilla bean.

In a large bowl, combine the sugar, cornstarch, cinnamon, ginger, pepper, and salt and stir to mix. Add the eggs, egg yolks, and sweet potato purée and whisk until combined. Slowly add about 1 cup of the warm milk mixture, whisking constantly, to temper the eggs. Whisk the egg mixture back into the remaining milk mixture in the saucepan and place back over medium-low heat. Continue to cook, whisking constantly, until the mixture thickens, 3–4 minutes. You want to see a few bubbles begin to rise slowly from the bottom of the pan. Do not let the mixture come to a full boil or cook too long—you will overcook the eggs. The mixture is thick enough when the whisk leaves tracks as you stir. Remove from the heat to stop the cooking process and strain through a mesh strainer into a large bowl. Add the butter and whisk until melted. Place a layer of plastic wrap directly on the custard and set aside to cool slightly.

Once the filling has cooled to room temperature, spread it evenly over the caramel layer and refrigerate the pie until firm, at least 2 hours or overnight.

For the topping: When ready to serve, place the heavy cream in a medium bowl and beat with an electric mixer on high speed until soft peaks form. Add the sugar and continue to beat just to combine. Remove the pie from the refrigerator. Top with the whipped cream, slice, and serve cold or refrigerate until ready to serve.

NOTE ✳ To make the sweet potato purée, preheat the oven to 400°. Wrap 1 large sweet potato in foil and bake for 50–60 minutes until very soft to the touch. Remove the foil; when cool enough to handle, slip the skin off. Place the sweet potato in the bowl of a food processor fitted with the metal blade and purée until smooth. One medium-large to large sweet potato makes about 1 cup of purée.

Icebox Pies

In the South, icebox pies got their name from where they were stored until served—in the icebox and, later, in the refrigerator. As far back as the 1930s the icebox pie was a revelation in the summertime for overheated southern cooks because of stove-top preparation or simply mixing and chilling instead of baking. Not heating up your kitchen on a hot summer day was a big plus during those years before everyone had air conditioning, especially in the South. All you need is to whip up a custard or mix a few ingredients into sweetened condensed milk, pour the filling into a graham cracker or other cookie crust, and place the pie in the refrigerator to chill for a few hours while you go about your day. The popularity of these pies exploded because they were the perfect quick, make-ahead dessert, cool and refreshing without a lot of fuss and effort. I think you'll find that these recipes become some of your favorites for all the same reasons.

Bill Smith's Atlantic Beach Pie
with Saltine Crust

I ate this pie for many years at Crook's Corner in Chapel Hill, North Carolina, trying to detect what made Bill Smith's pie so different from any other lemon icebox pie I had ever tasted. Finally, Bill told me it was in the salty cracker crumb crust made with saltines. He adapted the recipe from the original Atlantic Beach pie recipe he grew up on, topped with meringue. He replaced the meringue with whipped cream and coarse sea salt for garnish to complement the creamy tart filling. I would call this pie simple perfection, much like many things Bill makes at Crook's Corner. By the way, this pie does go into the oven briefly.

MAKES ONE 9-INCH PIE / SERVES 8–10

One 9-inch prebaked Saltine Cracker Crust (page 148)
1 (14-ounce) can sweetened condensed milk
4 large egg yolks, lightly beaten
½ cup juice from lemons, limes, or a mixture
For the topping
1 cup heavy cream
¼ cup granulated sugar
Coarse sea salt for garnish

Preheat the oven to 350°. Place the prepared crust on a rimmed baking sheet and set aside.

In a medium bowl, combine the condensed milk, egg yolks, and citrus juice, and whisk until well mixed. Pour the filling into the prepared crust.

Place on the center rack in the oven to bake for 15–16 minutes, until just set around the edges and slightly soft in the center. Remove from the oven, cool to room temperature, cover with plastic wrap, and refrigerate until firm, at least 4 hours or overnight.

For the topping: When ready to serve, pour the cream into a medium bowl and beat with an electric mixer on high speed until soft peaks form. Add the sugar and continue to beat just to combine. Remove the pie from the refrigerator. Top with the whipped cream, sprinkle with sea salt, slice, and serve cold.

Banana Chocolate Peanut Butter Pie

This is a banana cream pie on overload—with the addition of peanut butter and chocolate you can't go wrong. I have taken this pie to many dinner parties. With its creamy peanut butter chocolate layer beneath a layer of bananas and a heap of vanilla custard on top, it is a definite crowd pleaser.

MAKES ONE 9-INCH PIE / SERVES 8–10

One 9-inch prebaked Graham Cracker Crust (page 145)

FOR THE PEANUT CHOCOLATE LAYER

$\frac{1}{2}$ cup heavy cream
$\frac{1}{2}$ cup creamy peanut butter
$\frac{1}{2}$ cup semisweet chocolate chips

FOR THE BANANA CREAM LAYER

$1\frac{1}{2}$ cups milk
1 vanilla bean, split in half, seeds scraped
$\frac{1}{2}$ cup granulated sugar
3 tablespoons cornstarch
$\frac{1}{2}$ teaspoon kosher salt
3 large egg yolks
3 tablespoons unsalted butter, cut into small pieces
1 ripe banana

FOR THE TOPPING

1 cup heavy cream
$\frac{1}{4}$ cup granulated sugar
Peanuts and chocolate shavings for garnish

For the peanut chocolate layer: Pour the cream into a heavy-bottomed, non-aluminum saucepan over medium heat and bring to a boil. While the cream is coming to a boil, place the chocolate chips and peanut butter in a large bowl. Pour the boiling cream over the chocolate chips and peanut butter and whisk to blend until creamy. Spread the chocolate mixture in the bottom of the piecrust and refrigerate to chill.

For the banana cream layer: Meanwhile, place the milk in the same saucepan over medium heat. Add the vanilla bean and seeds and whisk to mix. Scald the milk, bringing it just to under a boil. The milk will start to bubble around the edges and steam.

In a separate large bowl, mix together the sugar, cornstarch, and salt. Add the egg yolks and whisk until combined. Slowly add about 1 cup of the warm milk mixture, whisking constantly, to temper the eggs. Whisk the egg mixture back into the remaining milk mixture in the saucepan and place back over medium-low heat. Continue to cook, whisking constantly, until the mixture thickens, 3–4 minutes more. You want to see a few bubbles begin to rise slowly from the bottom of the pan. Do not let the mixture come to a full boil or cook too long—you will overcook the eggs. The mixture is thick enough when the whisk leaves tracks as you stir. Immediately transfer the custard to a bowl to stop the cooking process. Remove the vanilla bean. Add the butter and whisk until melted. Place a layer of plastic wrap directly on the custard and set aside to cool to room temperature.

Thinly slice the banana and arrange over the chocolate layer of the pie. Spread the custard evenly over the banana layer and refrigerate until firm, at least 2 hours or overnight.

For the topping: When ready to serve, whip the cream with an electric mixer until soft peaks form. Add the sugar and mix to combine. Spread the whipped cream over the top of the pie. Sprinkle the top with salted peanuts and drizzle with melted chocolate or sprinkle with shaved chocolate. Refrigerate until ready to serve. Slice and serve chilled.

Cherry Cream Cheese Pie

We all grew up with this pie—this was considered cheesecake in my family. It was one of the first pies my newlywed sister learned to make from her mother-in-law, Bobbie, the mother of eight kids and not a lot of time for baking. This is what Bobbie's generation called a dump-and-go recipe. I have updated it by replacing the cherry pie filling with tart cherries and the sweetened condensed milk with crème fraîche. All of this, along with the gingersnap crust, gives it the perfect balance of sweet and tart.

MAKES ONE 9-INCH PIE / SERVES 8–10

One 9-inch prebaked Gingersnap Crust (page 147)

FOR THE CHERRY LAYER

2 cups stemmed, pitted sour cherries

½ cup granulated sugar

2 tablespoons cornstarch

FOR THE CREAM CHEESE LAYER

½ cup heavy cream

8 ounces (1 block) cream cheese, at room temperature

6 ounces crème fraîche

¾ cup confectioners' sugar

Finely grated zest and juice of 1 lemon

1 tablespoon pure vanilla extract

¼ teaspoon kosher salt

For the cherry layer: Place the cherries and granulated sugar in a saucepan over medium-high heat and bring to a low boil, stirring occasionally. Cook for about 10 minutes, stirring occasionally until the cherries are tender. Add the cornstarch to ¼ cup of water and stir to mix, then pour into the cherry mixture and bring to a low boil. Let boil about 1 minute more, stirring constantly, until the mixture thickens. Pour into a bowl and refrigerate to chill completely.

For the cream cheese layer: Beat the heavy cream in a large bowl with an electric mixer until stiff peaks form. Chill in the refrigerator while you make the remainder of the filling.

In a separate large bowl, beat the cream cheese and crème fraîche with an electric mixer until light and fluffy. Slowly sift in the confectioners' sugar until all is incorporated and smooth. Add the lemon zest and juice, vanilla, and salt and mix to combine.

Fold the whipped cream into the cream cheese mixture just to combine; do not over mix. Pour the filling into the prepared crust and refrigerate until firm, at least 3 hours or overnight.

When ready to serve, spoon the cherries in the center of the pie and spread, not covering the pie completely. Slice and serve chilled, with a dollop of whipped cream or crème fraîche if desired.

Indian River Citrus Pie

Key lime pie has always been one of my favorites, but the combination of lemons, limes, oranges, and grapefruit gives this pie the perfect blend of citrus. The inspiration for this pie came from a trip driving back from Florida with Peter in January and passing all the beautiful India River citrus stands along the side of the road. Since we were driving I had to take advantage and load the car up with Valencia, Navel, Temple, and Parson Brown oranges, Flame, Marsh, Duncan, and Ruby Red grapefruits, tangerines, tangelos, lemons, and limes. I encourage you to take advantage of all the winter citrus in your market; some of my other favorites are Cara Cara and blood oranges, Meyer lemons, clementines, and satsumas.

MAKES ONE 9-INCH PIE / SERVES 8–10

One 9-inch prebaked Gingersnap Crust (page 147)

FOR THE FILLING

Finely grated zest and juice with pulp from
    1 lemon, 1 lime, ½ orange, and ½ grapefruit
    (about 1 cup juice)
3 large eggs, lightly beaten
1 (14-ounce) can sweetened condensed milk
2 tablespoons finely chopped crystallized ginger
1 teaspoon pure vanilla extract
½ teaspoon kosher salt

FOR THE TOPPING

1 cup heavy cream
¼ cup granulated sugar
Crystallized ginger and citrus zest, for garnish

Preheat the oven to 325°. Place the prepared piecrust on a rimmed baking sheet and set aside.

For the filling: In a medium bowl, stir the citrus zest and juice and eggs together. Add the condensed milk, ginger, vanilla, and salt and whisk until combined.

Pour the filling into the prepared crust and place the pie on the center rack of the oven to bake for 15–20 minutes. It will still be loose in the center but slightly firm around the edges. Remove from the oven, cool to room temperature, cover with plastic wrap, and refrigerate until firm, at least 4 hours or overnight.

For the topping: When ready to serve, pour the cream into a medium bowl and beat with an electric mixer on high speed until soft peaks form. Add the sugar and continue to beat just to combine. Remove the pie from the refrigerator. Top with the whipped cream, garnish with julienned crystallized ginger and citrus zest, slice, and serve cold.

Crunchy Peanut Butter Pie

We can thank George Washington Carver for his research with peanuts in the early 1900s from which he developed approximately three hundred products using this legume. (A peanut is not actually a nut, and peanut butter contains neither nuts nor butter.) Though Carver did not develop peanut butter, there are many stories of how this American favorite originated. What made peanut butter a national sensation was its introduction at the St. Louis World's Fair in 1904. Since then our love affair with peanut butter has not cooled—Americans consume more than eight hundred million dollars' worth of peanut butter annually. You can add just about anything sweet to peanut butter, and it also goes well with bananas, chocolate, and caramel. I like the crunchy, salty addition of peanut brittle to this pie, added at the last minute to keep the crunch.

MAKES ONE 9-INCH PIE / SERVES 8–10

One 9-inch prebaked Black Bottom Crust (page 146)
  or Graham Cracker Crust (page 145)

FOR THE FILLING
8 ounces (1 block) cream cheese, at room temperature
1 cup creamy peanut butter, at room temperature
1 (14-ounce) can sweetened condensed milk
1 teaspoon pure vanilla extract
½ teaspoon kosher salt
½ cup heavy cream

FOR THE TOPPING
½ cup chopped peanut brittle, plus more for garnish
1 cup heavy cream
¼ cup granulated sugar

For the filling: Cream the cream cheese and peanut butter in a large bowl with an electric mixer or a wooden spoon until soft and creamy. Add the condensed milk and beat until thoroughly blended. Add the vanilla and salt and stir to mix.

In a separate bowl with an electric mixer, whip the cream to stiff peaks. Gently fold the whipped cream into the peanut butter mixture. Spoon the mixture into the prepared piecrust, spread evenly, and refrigerate until firm, at least 1 hour or overnight.

For the topping: When ready to serve, remove the pie from the refrigerator and sprinkle the peanut brittle over the top. Place the heavy cream in a medium bowl and beat with an electric mixer on high speed until soft peaks form. Add the sugar and continue to beat just to combine. Top with the whipped cream, garnish with additional chopped peanut brittle, slice, and serve cold.

Say's Fresh Peach Pie
with Cream Cheese Cake Crust

I wish I knew where this recipe came from. I think my mother made it up from all her favorite things: cream cheese, peaches, and sugar. It's a combination of peach shortcake and pie, but I guarantee that you will find it one of best pies you've ever made. There are two keys to making this pie perfect. First, you need really good ripe peaches; if they are not ripe, let them sit a few days to ripen. Second, do not overbake the crust; it should be very soft, almost gooey.

MAKES ONE 9-INCH PIE / SERVES 8–10

FOR THE CRUST

8 tablespoons (1 stick) unsalted butter, at room
    temperature
8 ounces (1 block) cream cheese, cut into small pieces,
    at room temperature
1¼ cups granulated sugar
2 teaspoons pure vanilla extract
1¼ cups self-rising flour

FOR THE FILLING

6–7 cups ripe peaches (about 3 pounds)
½–¾ cup granulated sugar, depending on the
    sweetness of the fruit
Juice of 1 lemon

FOR THE TOPPING

1 cup heavy cream
¼ cup granulated sugar

For the crust: Preheat the oven to 350°. Lightly grease a 9-inch pie pan and place it on a rimmed baking sheet.

Cream the butter, cream cheese, and sugar in the bowl of a stand mixer and beat with the paddle until smooth. Alternately, place in a large bowl and cream together with a wooden spoon. Add the vanilla and stir to mix. Slowly add the flour just until all is incorporated and there are no visible signs of dry ingredients. The dough will be sticky.

Spread the dough into the bottom of the prepared pan and pat with lightly floured hands to even it out. Place on the center rack in the oven to bake for about 20 minutes, rotating halfway through, until puffy and golden brown around the edges and still soft in the center. Remove from the oven and cool completely before adding the fruit.

For the filling: Meanwhile peel, pit, and slice the peaches over a large bowl to collect the juice. Add the sugar and lemon juice and stir to combine so that the peaches release their juice.

Pour the peaches and juice over the top of the piecrust and spread in an even layer to cover the crust. Cover with plastic wrap and refrigerate until ready to serve. This pie is best if it has time to sit a few hours before serving: the peach juices soak into the crust.

For the topping: Pour the cream into a medium bowl and beat with an electric mixer on high speed until soft peaks form. Add the sugar and continue to beat just to combine. Remove the pie from the refrigerator. Top with the whipped cream, slice, and serve cold.

Raspberry Fool Semifreddo Pie

With its light, airy texture and flavor of fresh raspberries with a hint of lemon, this is the prefect dessert to follow a big meal. For easy entertaining, make it several days in advance and store in your freezer.

MAKES ONE 9-INCH PIE / SERVES 8–10

One 9-inch prebaked Black Bottom Crust (page 146)
   or Gingersnap Crust (page 147)
2 large eggs
¾ cup granulated sugar, divided
3 cups fresh raspberries (or combination with blackberries),
   plus more for garnish
Finely grated zest and juice of 1 lemon
1 cup heavy cream

Beat the eggs and ½ cup of the sugar in a large heatproof bowl with an electric mixer on high until doubled in size and pale yellow, 3–4 minutes. Set the bowl over a saucepan with about 1 inch of simmering water (do not let the bowl touch the water) and continue to beat until the custard thickens, about 4 minutes or until an instant-read thermometer registers 140°F. Transfer the mixture to another bowl and refrigerate to chill, stirring occasionally.

Once the custard is cool, toss the raspberries with the lemon zest and juice and the remaining sugar and give them a rough mash. Set the raspberries aside to release their juice.

Whip the cream to stiff peaks and gently fold the cream into the custard to combine. Fold in the raspberries and their juice, leaving streaks of berries so that the mixture is not completely combined. Spoon the filling into the prepared crust and place in the freezer until slightly firm on top, about 30 minutes. Remove from the freezer and cover with plastic wrap, then place back in the freezer until completely firm, at least 3 hours or overnight.

When ready to serve, remove from the freezer 5–10 minutes before slicing. Serve chilled with fresh raspberries on top.

Tarts, Hand Pies, and Others

By definition, a tart is not a tart if no tart pan is used, but in my book a tart can take many forms. I grouped these recipes together because they are all fun to make. They can be made large, small, or miniature, free-form or rolled to the shape of a pan, round, rectangular, or square. Traditionally made with a light base of pastry cream in a crisp, buttery crust and topped with fresh fruit, these tarts are best eaten the day they are made. In this chapter I give you different versions of the traditional fresh fruit tart, some made with filling that requires no cooking or baking, some made with brown butter or ground nuts. You'll find individual hand pies, baked or fried to your liking, and rustic galettes and crostatas filled with seasonal plums, figs, and berries, bursting with flavor. Whether you get out your tart pans and make one of these delicate fruit tarts in a crisp shell or roll a rustic, free-form tart that is baked directly on a sheet pan, you will enjoy the fruits of the season.

Aunt Betty's Blueberry Tart

I'm not sure whose Aunt Betty this is, but this recipe came to me from a friend of a friend in Lake Placid, New York, where I spend the summer and blueberries are plentiful all summer long. Her original recipe for the crust is made from Bisquick, but I like the crisp Sweet Tart Crust with the combination of the sour cream, currant jelly, and blueberries.

MAKES ONE 9- OR 10-INCH TART / SERVES 8–10

½ recipe prebaked (page 17) Sweet Tart Crust (page 134)

FOR THE FILLING
1 (8-ounce) jar red currant jelly, at room temperature
3–4 cups fresh blueberries, washed and drained
1 cup sour cream

FOR THE TOPPING
1 cup heavy cream
¼ cup granulated sugar

Remove the crust from the tart pan and place it on a large plate or platter.

For the filling: Warm the jelly in the microwave slightly to a spreadable but not liquid consistency. Spoon the jelly over the bottom of the prepared crust and spread evenly. Sprinkle the blueberries on top, slightly pressing them down into the jelly. Spread an even layer of sour cream over the berries. Cover with plastic wrap and refrigerate for at least 30 minutes.

For the topping: When ready to serve, pour the cream into a medium bowl and beat with an electric mixer on high speed until soft peaks form. Add the sugar and continue to beat just to combine. Remove the tart from the refrigerator. Top with the whipped cream, slice, and serve cold.

Granny Foster's Fried Apple Pies

I loved staying at my grandparents' farm when I was young. One of my fondest memories is having fried apple pies for breakfast. In the fall, when apples were plentiful, my grandmother made these pies from apples right off her tree. Extra apples were picked for making applesauce to enjoy these delightful pies year-round. There were several recipes in her book for fried pies; this one had a handwritten note on it that read, "Mrs. Cherry makes this with peaches from her tree she dries in the sun." Fried pies have recently popped up on restaurant menus across the South, from pocket pies at Butcher in New Orleans, where the flavors change with the seasons, to strawberries and moonshine from Grits & Groceries in Belton, South Carolina. This recipe is easier to work with if you make the apple filling ahead of time and chill it. The filling stays in place and does not ooze from the edges when the pies are fried.

MAKES EIGHT 6-INCH PIES

FOR THE FILLING

6 cups peeled, cored, and chopped tart and sweet apples
(5–6 apples)
3/4 cups granulated sugar, plus more for sprinkling on top
Finely grated zest and juice of 1 lemon
2 teaspoons pure vanilla extract
1/2 teaspoon kosher salt
1/4 teaspoon allspice
2 tablespoons (1/4 stick) unsalted butter

FOR THE DOUGH

3 cups self-rising flour
1/2 teaspoon kosher salt
8 tablespoons cold lard or vegetable shortening
1/2–3/4 cup cold milk
Egg wash made with 1 egg whisked with 1 tablespoon milk
Vegetable oil for frying

For the filling: Combine the apples, sugar, lemon zest and juice, vanilla, salt, and allspice in a medium saucepan and bring to a low boil over medium heat. Reduce the heat to low and simmer until the apples release their juice and start to come apart but are still chunky and the mixture is slightly thick, 10–15 minutes, stirring occasionally. If the apples are not releasing juice, add about ⅓ cup water or apple juice to the pan.

Remove from the heat and stir in the butter until melted. Remove the mixture from the pan and place in a bowl, cover, and refrigerate for at least 1 hour or overnight.

For the dough: In a large bowl, stir together the flour and salt. Mix in the lard or shortening with a pastry blender or fork until the mixture resembles coarse meal.

Add the milk about ¼ cup at a time, mixing well until the dough comes together but is not sticky. Divide the dough in half and shape each piece into a flat, round disk. Cover with plastic wrap and refrigerate for at least 1 hour or overnight.

Divide each round into 4 equal pieces and roll each into a 7-inch circle about ⅛ inch thick. Trim the edges to make a 6-inch circle. Refrigerate the rounds while rolling the remaining pieces.

To assemble: Working with 2–3 pies at once, place them on a rimmed baking sheet and brush the outer edges of the rounds with the egg wash. Place about 2 heaping tablespoons of the filling in the middle of the right side of each round, not going all the way to the edge. Fold the left side of the dough over to make a half-moon shape. Fold or crimp the edges together firmly, with the tines of a fork, making sure no filling is leaking from the edges. Refrigerate while working on the other pies. Repeat with the remaining pies and chill for about 30 minutes.

When ready to cook, heat just enough oil to cover the bottom of a large skillet about ¼ inch deep over medium-high heat until sizzling hot. Gently add the pies, 3–4 at a time, not to overcrowd the skillet. Reduce the heat to medium and cook for 2–3 minutes per side, turning only once, until the dough is crisp and golden brown on both sides. Place on a wire rack over a baking sheet to drain. While the pies are still warm, sprinkle with sugar to dust the outside. Repeat with the remaining pies, adding more oil as needed. Cool slightly and serve warm straight from the hand or on a plate with a scoop of vanilla ice cream.

Green Tomato Apple Crostata

Green tomatoes are a summer staple in the South, but we do have ways of preparing them other than the traditional fried green tomatoes. My grandmother's green tomato relish made use of the end-of-summer green tomatoes still on the vine that would not ripen before the first frost. This is one of my favorite ways to make use of the early fall apples and those last tomatoes that do not have time to ripen.

MAKES ONE 9- TO 10-INCH CROSTATA / SERVES 8–10

½ recipe Hand Pie Crust (page 142)

2 medium green tomatoes, cored

1 tablespoon kosher salt

½ cup plus 2 tablespoons granulated sugar, divided

2–3 tart apples, cored, peeled, and thinly sliced
   (such as Granny Smith, Jonathan, or Arkansas Black)

½ cup golden raisins

3 tablespoons all-purpose flour

Finely grated zest and juice of 1 lemon

½ teaspoon ground cinnamon

½ teaspoon ground ginger

3 tablespoons unsalted butter, cut into small pieces

Egg wash made with 1 egg whisked with 1 tablespoon milk

Roll the dough into a 12-inch round and place on parchment paper on a rimmed baking sheet. Chill in the refrigerator.

Slice the tomatoes in half, from top to bottom. Slice each half into ¼-inch-thick slices and place in a colander. Sprinkle with the salt and 1 tablespoon of the sugar and drain for about 30 minutes. Remove from the colander, spread in an even layer on a plate lined with paper towels, and blot the tops with more paper towels.

Place the tomatoes and apples in a large bowl, then add the raisins, ½ cup of the sugar, flour, lemon zest and juice, cinnamon, and ginger and stir to mix thoroughly. Spoon the tomato-apple mixture into the center of the pie dough and spread evenly, leaving about 2 inches around the edges. Dot the fruit with butter and brush the rim with the egg wash. Fold the edges up around to form a rim around the filling, pressing gently to adhere. Brush the outside with the egg wash and sprinkle all over with the remaining sugar. Chill in the refrigerator for about 30 minutes.

Preheat the oven to 375°.

Place the crostata on the center rack in the oven to bake for 50–55 minutes, until the filling is bubbling and the crust is golden brown. If the crust starts browning too quickly, cover with foil until the apples are tender. Remove from the oven and cool about 1 hour before slicing. Serve warm or at room temperature with a dollop of crème fraîche.

Cherry Berry Crostatas

This classic Italian tart dates back to 1570, when Bartolomeo Scappi included a recipe for a plum and sour cherry crostata in his cookbook Opera dell'arte del cucinare. *During the summer I make it with most any type of fruit in the market at the time: peaches, plums, apples, or berries. It is one of the easiest tarts to throw together, and I usually make extra to have the next day for breakfast. I make individual tarts, but this recipe can easily be made as one large tart—just adjust the cooking time.*

MAKES 8 INDIVIDUAL 4- TO 5-INCH CROSTATAS

1 recipe Hand Pie Crust (page 142), rolled in log form instead of flat, round disks

3 cups mixed berries, raspberries, blueberries, strawberries, and blackberries

2 cups tart cherries, stems removed and pitted

½ cup granulated sugar, plus more for sprinkling on top

3 tablespoons cornstarch

1 teaspoon ground cinnamon

½ teaspoon ground ginger

¼ teaspoon kosher salt

4 tablespoons (½ stick) unsalted butter, cut into 8 pieces

Egg wash made with 1 egg whisked with 1 tablespoon milk

Lightly grease 2 large baking sheets or line with parchment paper.

Remove the dough from the refrigerator and divide it into 8 equal pieces. On a lightly floured surface, roll each piece into a 6-inch round and place on the prepared baking sheets. Chill in the refrigerator while you make the filling.

In a large bowl, combine the berries, cherries, sugar, cornstarch, cinnamon, ginger, and salt and toss to mix.

Scoop about ½ cup of the fruit mixture into the center of each round, dividing evenly. Top each with a piece of butter and fold about 1 inch of the dough over the fruit all the way around to form a rim. Brush the outside of each tart with the egg wash. Sprinkle with sugar and refrigerate for 30 minutes to chill the dough (this helps the sides stay up around the fruit and not collapse).

Preheat the oven to 375°.

Place the baking sheets on the center racks in the oven to bake for 35–40 minutes, rotating and reversing the pans' positions halfway through, until golden brown and the fruit is bubbling. Remove from the oven and cool slightly. Serve warm or at room temperature, topped with homemade ice cream or lightly sweetened whipped cream.

Fig Pecan Frangipane Tart

The fig tree at Foster's Market is iconic; we planted it in 1990, the year we opened the market. We moved it in 1995 when we expanded, and I thought for sure we were going to lose it because in five years it had grown to an enormous size. We cut it back almost to the ground, moved it over a few yards, and replanted it, and it came back bigger than ever. Now it takes up half our side yard and gives us many, many figs each year (if we can keep the neighbors from taking them). If you come to the market in mid- to late summer, you are sure to find figs on our menu and on the tree. This is one of those desserts that is not overly sweet, and the pecans go perfectly with the figs, combining two of our most cherished southern treasures.

MAKES ONE 9- OR 10-INCH TART / SERVES 8–10

One 9- or 10-inch parbaked (pages 16–17) Sweet Tart Crust
   (page 134)
1½ cup roughly chopped pecans
½ cup granulated sugar, plus more for sprinkling on top
2 large eggs
5 tablespoons unsalted butter, at room temperature
1 tablespoon bourbon
2 teaspoons pure vanilla extract
½ teaspoon kosher salt
Finely grated zest and juice of 1 lemon
8–10 fresh figs, stemmed, quartered

Preheat the oven to 375°. Place the prepared tart shell on a rimmed baking sheet and set aside.

In a food processor, finely grind the pecans and sugar until the mixture resembles coarse meal. Add the eggs, butter, bourbon, vanilla, salt, and lemon zest and juice, and purée until smooth and blended.

Spread the filling over the bottom of the crust; arrange the figs cut-side up over the top in a circular pattern, pressing gently into the filling. Sprinkle generously with about 1 tablespoon sugar. Place on the center rack in the oven and bake for 40–45 minutes, rotating halfway through, until center is set and the top is golden and slightly puffy. Remove from the oven and cool slightly before serving. Serve warm or at room temperature.

Roasted Pear Brown Butter Tart

Some of my favorite pears for baking are Bosc, Bartlett, and Anjou. The pears should give just a little when touched but not feel soft, and will bake to a tender ripeness. This is the perfect dessert to serve after a big meal. I usually make it for Thanksgiving and Christmas, just a little slice of something sweet to end a perfect meal.

MAKES ONE 9- OR 10-INCH TART / SERVES 8–10

One 9- or 10-inch parbaked (pages 16–17) Sweet Tart Crust (page 134)
2 pears, peeled, cut into quarters and cored
$\frac{1}{2}$ cup light brown sugar
Juice of 1 lemon
1 tablespoon pure vanilla extract
5 tablespoons unsalted butter
1 vanilla bean
2 large egg yolks
1 large egg
$\frac{3}{4}$ cup granulated sugar, plus more for sprinkling on top
Finely grated zest and juice of $\frac{1}{2}$ lemon
2 tablespoons all-purpose flour
$\frac{1}{2}$ teaspoon kosher salt

Preheat the oven to 400°. Place the prepared crust on a rimmed baking sheet and set aside.

In a medium bowl, toss the pears with the brown sugar, lemon juice, and vanilla. Place on a separate rimmed sheet pan and spread evenly, scraping out the sugar mixture over and around the pears. Roast in the oven until the pears and sugar are caramelized, 35–40 minutes, stirring halfway through. Remove from the oven and set aside to cool slightly. Reduce the oven temperature to 375°.

Meanwhile, place the butter in a small saucepan over medium heat. Split the vanilla bean in half and scrape out the seeds, then add the seeds and the bean to the butter. Cook, swirling the pan often, just until the butter turns light brown and releases a nutty fragrance, 2–3 minutes. Remove from the heat immediately and transfer to a bowl to stop the cooking process. Cool slightly.

With an electric mixer, beat the egg yolks, egg, and sugar until light and fluffy, stopping to scrape down the bowl several times, about 3 minutes. Slowly add the butter and mix well. Add the lemon zest and juice, flour, and salt and stir to mix.

Spread the filling evenly over the bottom of the prepared tart shell. Place the pears on top in a circular pattern with the caramelized side up. Place on the center rack in the oven and bake for 30–35 minutes, until the filling puffs up and is firm. Remove from the oven and cool about 1 hour before serving. Serve warm with lightly sweetened whipped cream or crème fraîche.

Meyer Lemon Swiss Meringue Tart

My love for Meyer lemons goes way back. I even have a Meyer lemon tree. If you haven't tried a Meyer lemon, it's time you do so. Their season is usually around December through late spring. They are sweeter than other lemons, and the rind has its own distinctive herbal, spicy quality. They taste like a cross between a regular lemon and a mandarin orange, making this tart a little sweeter than a traditional lemon tart. This creamy curd is a labor of love but well worth the effort. It can be made several days in advance and stored refrigerated in an airtight container until ready to use.

MAKES ONE 9- OR 10-INCH TART / SERVES 8–10

One 9- or 10-inch prebaked (page 17) Sweet Tart Crust
(page 134)

FOR THE FILLING

1 cup granulated sugar

2 large eggs

4 large egg yolks

Finely grated zest and juice of 3 Meyer lemons
(about $\frac{1}{2}$ cup juice)

$\frac{1}{2}$ teaspoon kosher salt

8 tablespoons (1 stick) unsalted butter,
cut into small pieces

1 teaspoon pure vanilla extract

FOR THE TOPPING

4 large egg whites

$\frac{3}{4}$ cup granulated sugar

$\frac{1}{4}$ teaspoon kosher salt

For the filling: In a heatproof bowl, whisk together the sugar, eggs, egg yolks, lemon zest and juice, and salt. Place the bowl over a pot of simmering water, making sure the bottom of the bowl does not touch the water. Stir the mixture with a wooden spoon or whisk, 15–18 minutes, until it thickens to coat the back of the spoon and is the consistency of pudding. You must stir constantly or the eggs will overcook.

Remove the bowl from the heat and whisk in the butter, a few pieces at a time, until melted and incorporated. Add the vanilla and whisk to combine. Pour the mixture into the cooled shell and spread evenly. Place a layer of plastic wrap directly on the custard and refrigerate for several hours.

For the topping: When ready to serve, place the egg whites, sugar, and salt in a large heatproof bowl over a pot of simmering water, making sure the bottom of the bowl does not touch the water. Whisk constantly until the sugar dissolves and the whites are hot, 3–5 minutes.

Remove from the heat and beat with an electric mixer on medium speed until soft peaks form, 1–2 minutes. Increase the speed to high and continue to beat until stiff, glossy peaks form, 2–3 minutes more. You will know they are ready if the tips of the meringue curl over when the beater is lifted and the meringue does not slide around in the bowl. (If the egg whites start to break apart or release a clear liquid, you have gone too far; start over and consider it practice.)

Pipe the meringue over the top of the tart in a decorative pattern. Using a kitchen torch, lightly brown the tips of the meringue, or briefly run the tart under a preheated broiler (do not leave unattended: the tips will brown quickly). Slice and serve soon after the meringue has been toasted. Do not refrigerate after the meringue has been added. This tart does not keep well in the refrigerator.

Vanilla Peach Black Pepper Hand Pies

This is my version of those delicious Granny Foster's Fried Apple Pies, without all the trouble of frying. If you like spicy, add a little more black pepper and 2 tablespoons of chopped crystallized ginger into the filling along with the other spices. Hand pies work well with sweet and savory fillings, including baked pumpkin, sweet potatoes, and butternut squash, apples, pears, and berries, or a combination.

MAKES EIGHT 6-INCH HAND PIES

1 recipe Hand Pie Crust (page 142), rolled into a log to chill

6–7 peaches, peeled, pitted, and chopped (4–5 cups)

½ cup granulated sugar, plus more for sprinkling on top

2 tablespoons quick-cooking tapioca

1 tablespoon pure vanilla extract

Finely grated zest of 1 lemon

1 teaspoon freshly ground black pepper

½ teaspoon ground ginger

½ teaspoon freshly grated nutmeg

½ teaspoon kosher salt

Egg wash made with 1 egg whisked with 1 tablespoon milk

2 tablespoons (¼ stick) unsalted butter, cut into 8 pieces

Lightly grease 2 rimmed baking sheets or line with parchment paper.

Divide the dough into 8 equal pieces and roll each into a 6- to 7-inch circle about ⅛ inch thick. Trim the edges to make even circles. Chill in the refrigerator while you make the filling.

In a large bowl, combine the peaches and any juice that collected when you peeled them with the sugar, tapioca, vanilla, lemon zest, black pepper, ginger, nutmeg, and salt and stir to mix.

Working with 2–3 pies at once, place the dough circles on a rimmed baking sheet and brush the outer edges with the egg wash. Place 2 heaping tablespoons of the filling on the center of the right side of each round, leaving a rim around the edges. Top each with a piece of the butter and fold the left side of the dough over to make a half-moon shape. Fold or crimp the edges together firmly, making sure that no filling is leaking from the edges. Chill in the refrigerator while forming the remaining pies. Refrigerate for about 30 minutes before baking.

When ready to bake, preheat the oven to 375°. Place the hand pies on the prepared pans. Make vents in the top of each hand pie with a paring knife or tines of a fork, brush with the remaining egg wash, and sprinkle with sugar. Place on the center racks in the oven and bake for 25–30 minutes, rotating and reversing the pans' positions halfway through, until golden brown and the filling is bubbling through the top of the pies. Remove from the oven and cool slightly before serving warm or completely cooled.

Plum Frangipane Galette

I find Italian plums, deep purple with yellow flesh, the best for baking because they hold their shape when baked. The plum's tart and juicy flavor is perfect for the creamy almond frangipane filling. This recipe also works well with peaches, cherries, or figs.

MAKES ONE 9- OR 10-INCH GALETTE / SERVES 8–10

½ recipe Hand Pie Crust (page 142)

1 cup sliced blanched almonds

½ cup granulated sugar, plus more for sprinkling on top

2 large eggs

5 tablespoons unsalted butter, cut into small pieces,
    at room temperature

½ teaspoon almond extract

½ teaspoon kosher salt

Finely grated zest and juice of 1 lemon

6–8 fresh plums, stemmed, cut in half, pit removed

Egg wash made with 1 egg whisked with 1 tablespoon milk

On a lightly floured surface, roll the dough into a 12-inch circle about ⅛ inch thick. Place on a rimmed baking sheet and chill in the refrigerator.

In a food processor, finely grind the almonds and sugar until the mixture resembles coarse meal. Add the eggs, butter, almond extract, salt, and lemon zest and juice and purée until smooth and blended.

Remove the dough from the refrigerator and spread the filling over the bottom, leaving about 2 inches around the edges. Arrange the plums cut-side up over the top of the filling in a circular pattern, pressing gently into the filling. Fold the edge of the dough over the fruit all the way around to form a rim. Brush the outside with the egg wash and sprinkle generously with about 1 tablespoon sugar. Chill in the refrigerator for about 30 minutes.

Preheat the oven to 375°.

Remove the galette from the refrigerator and place on the bottom rack in the oven to bake for 20 minutes. Move to the middle rack of the oven, rotate the pan, and continue to bake for 15–20 minutes, until center is set and the crust golden brown. Set aside to cool for about 1 hour before serving. Serve warm or at room temperature with lightly sweetened whipped cream or crème fraîche.

Springtime Strawberry Tart

My grandparents had a strawberry patch on their farm in Ten-
nessee; we would get out of school for a few days every spring to
pick strawberries. Visit a pick-your-own berry farm near you so
that you can pick ripe strawberries, since strawberries don't get
any sweeter after they are picked. This is the recipe I make when
ripe berries are available and I don't want to labor over the stove
making pastry cream or heat up the oven to make a fruit pie. The
quick and easy filling for the tart can be whipped up in minutes.
You can also make it ahead of time and refrigerate until ready to
use. This tart is also great with blueberries, blackberries, or rasp-
berries.

MAKES ONE 9- OR 10-INCH TART / SERVES 8–10

One 9- or 10-inch prebaked (page 17) Sweet Tart Crust
(page 134)

$1/2$ cup mascarpone cheese

$1/2$ cup sour cream

$1/4$ cup light brown sugar

2 teaspoons pure vanilla extract

$1/4$ teaspoon kosher salt

1 cup homemade or good-quality strawberry jam

1 quart ripe strawberries, capped and sliced

In a large bowl, stir the mascarpone and sour cream to combine thoroughly. Stir in the brown sugar, vanilla, and salt and refrigerate until ready to use. (The mixture can be refrigerated for up to 3 days at this point.)

Spread about ¾ of the jam evenly over the bottom of the tart shell. Top with the mascarpone mixture and spread evenly. Arrange the strawberries over the mascarpone mixture in a decorative overlapping pattern. Place the remaining jam in the microwave about 30 seconds to loosen and become slightly liquid. Brush the jam over the berries to glaze. Place in the refrigerator until ready to serve. This tart needs nothing more. Slice and serve chilled.

Savory Pies

When I was old enough to be trusted to turn the oven on by myself, I knew how to make one thing for dinner. I would take Mrs. Sullivan's Chicken Pot Pie out of the freezer and pop it in the oven. In no time I would have a plate of tender chunks of chicken in a creamy sauce topped with crusty pastry. (I could work around the peas and carrots.) I still love the simple pleasures of a one-dish meal, and a savory pie is the perfect such dish, anytime of the year. Whether it's a slice of tomato or crab pie in the summer, a sausage and sweet potato hand pie for a fall outing, or a chicken pot pie hot out of the oven, these are the comfort foods I grew up on and still crave. Make these savory pies the way you like—throw in a handful of spinach or kale, substitute turkey or chicken sausage for pork, add extra onion or cheese, a few herbs or some hot sauce. Use these recipes as guidelines and don't be afraid to give them your personal touch—who knows, you might become the next Mrs. Sullivan.

Chorizo Apple Sweet Potato Hand Pies

This surprising twist on the classic sausage apple pie is similar to an empanada made with a cornmeal cream cheese crust. The sweet, mellow flavors of the sweet potato and apple completely balance the spiciness of the chorizo. You can serve these hand pies warm or at room temperature, and they travel well, making them perfect for picnics or tailgating. They can also be made smaller to serve as appetizers or hors d'oeuvres.

MAKES EIGHT 6-INCH HAND PIES

---

1 recipe Cornmeal Cream Cheese Piecrust (page 138)
　or Pâte Brisée Piecrust (page 132)
1 tablespoon olive oil
2 tablespoons (¼ stick) unsalted butter
½ pound ground chorizo sausage
1 medium sweet potato, peeled and chopped
1 shallot, minced
1 tart apple, peeled, cored, and chopped
2 tablespoons all-purpose flour
1 tablespoon chopped fresh sage
2 teaspoons chopped fresh thyme
Kosher salt and freshly ground black pepper, to taste
1 cup chicken broth
7–8 kale leaves, stems removed and roughly chopped
Egg wash made with 1 large egg whisked with
　1 tablespoon milk

Preheat the oven to 375°.

Remove the dough from the refrigerator and divide each piece of dough into 4 equal pieces. On a lightly floured surface, roll each into a 7-inch circle about ⅛ inch thick. Trim the edges to make a 6-inch circle. Chill in the refrigerator while making the filling.

In a large skillet, heat the olive oil and butter over medium heat until sizzling. Add the sausage, breaking it up as it cooks, and sweet potatoes, stirring frequently, 5–6 minutes, until lightly browned. Add the shallots and apples and cook, stirring often, 2–3 minutes more. Add the flour, sage, thyme, salt, and pepper and cook and stir about 2 minutes until the flour cooks. Slowly add the broth and stir to mix. Add the kale and continue to cook just until the liquid thickens and the kale wilts, about 3 minutes more, stirring occasionally. Remove from the heat and set aside to cool.

Remove the rounds from the refrigerator and place on 1 or 2 rimmed baking sheets lined with parchment paper or lightly greased. Place about 2 heaping tablespoons of the filling on the right side of each round, leaving a ½-inch border.

Brush the edges of the rounds with the egg wash and fold the left side of the dough over the filling so that the edges meet and enclose the filling. Crimp the edges with a fork or your fingers to seal. Cut small vents in the top of each pie with a paring knife or prick with a fork.

Brush the tops with the remaining egg wash and sprinkle with salt. Place on the center rack in the oven to bake for 25–30 minutes, rotating halfway through, until golden brown and the filling is bubbling through the vents in the top. Remove from the oven and cool slightly before serving warm or at room temperature.

Judy's Summer Tomato Pie

When I was testing recipes for this book, everyone had "the best" tomato pie recipe they wanted to share. As I worked my way through them I realized they were all similar. This recipe is a combination of one from my sister Judy and one from my friend Josh. I added the cornbread crumbs that give it that extra crunch on top. The key to making this pie is using your favorite summer vine-ripened tomatoes.

MAKES ONE 9-INCH PIE / SERVES 6–8

One 9-inch parbaked (pages 16–17) Cornmeal Cream Cheese
   Piecrust (page 138) or Everyday Flaky Piecrust (page 130)
$\frac{1}{4}$ cup cornbread crumbs, divided (see Note)
2 large, ripe garden tomatoes (about 2 pounds),
   cored and sliced $\frac{1}{4}$ inch thick
Kosher salt for sprinkling the tomatoes
2 teaspoons olive oil
1 small onion, diced
1 cup grated sharp cheddar cheese
$\frac{1}{2}$ cup grated Parmesan cheese
$\frac{3}{4}$ cup mayonnaise
1 large egg, lightly beaten
1 tablespoon Dijon mustard
2 teaspoon hot sauce
$\frac{1}{4}$ cup thinly sliced fresh basil, plus more for garnish
$\frac{1}{2}$ teaspoon kosher salt
$\frac{1}{4}$ teaspoon freshly ground black pepper
$\frac{1}{8}$ teaspoon ground cayenne pepper

Preheat the oven to 350°.

Place the prepared crust on a rimmed baking sheet and sprinkle the bottom of the crust with 2 tablespoons of the cornbread crumbs.

Line a rimmed baking sheet with paper towels and spread the tomatoes on top in a single layer. Sprinkle generously with salt and set aside to drain for about 15 minutes.

Meanwhile, heat a skillet over medium heat, add the olive oil, and heat until sizzling. Add the onions and cook, stirring, for about 2 minutes, until the onions are soft; set aside to cool slightly.

In a medium bowl, combine the cheddar, Parmesan, mayonnaise, egg, mustard, and hot sauce and stir to mix.

Blot the tops of the tomatoes with paper towels, layer in the bottom of the piecrust, and sprinkle with basil, salt, black pepper, and cayenne pepper. Top with the onions and spoon the cheese mixture over the top, spreading evenly. Sprinkle with additional basil and the remaining bread crumbs.

Place on the center rack in the oven to bake for 35–40 minutes, rotating halfway through, until the pastry is golden brown and the pie is set and slightly puffy. Remove from the oven and cool to room temperature, about 30 minutes, before slicing. Serve warm or at room temperature with a tossed green salad.

NOTE ❋ To make the cornbread crumbs, crumble a day-old piece of cornbread on a rimmed baking sheet and sprinkle it with kosher salt and freshly ground black pepper. Drizzle lightly with olive oil and toss to mix. Place in a preheated 350° oven and toast until light brown around the edges of the pan and slightly dry, 5–10 minutes. Remove from the oven and allow to cool completely before storing in an airtight container until ready to use.

Caramelized Vidalia Onion and Roasted Tomato Tart with Whipped Feta

Vidalia, Georgia, and its surrounding counties have become world famous for onions, thanks to a farmer named Moses Coleman and the local soil. In 1931 Coleman was surprised to find that the onions he had planted were sweet instead of hot. A hard sell in the beginning, they soon became so popular that Georgia named the Vidalia onion its state vegetable in 1990. Over the years I have made many versions of this tart, using everything from fennel to turnip greens. This light, buttery pastry adapts to just about any filling; just don't overfill it, so that the pastry stays crispy. It is also great with the addition of prosciutto or crispy bacon, and it makes a perfect summer lunch.

MAKES ONE 6 × 12-INCH TART / SERVES 6–8

FOR THE CRUST
½ recipe Rough Puff Pastry (page 136)
Egg wash made with 1 large egg whisked with
    1 tablespoon milk

FOR THE WHIPPED FETA
6 ounces feta cheese, crumbled, at room temperature
6 ounces cream cheese, at room temperature

FOR THE FILLING
2 tablespoons olive oil, divided
1 tablespoon unsalted butter
1 small Vidalia onion, thinly sliced
Kosher salt and freshly ground black pepper, to taste
1 tablespoon balsamic vinegar
3 tablespoons fresh thyme leaves, divided
1 teaspoon granulated sugar
1 pint mixed cherry or grape tomatoes

Preheat the oven to 400°. Line a rimmed baking sheet with parchment paper and set aside.

Remove the dough from the refrigerator. On a lightly floured surface, roll the puff pastry into a 9 × 12-inch rectangle. Cut about ⅓ of the sheet off from the right side and cut this piece lengthwise into 4 equal strips.

To make a rim, brush the edges of the rectangle with the egg wash and place the strips of cut pastry along the outside edges and across the ends, trimming the ends as needed. Press gently to adhere. Place back in the refrigerator to chill.

For the whipped feta: Place the feta and cream cheese in the bowl of a food processor fitted with the metal blade and pulse 8–10 times until the cream cheese breaks up and blends with the feta. With the motor running, purée until completely smooth and creamy, stopping to scrape down the bowl several times during the process. Store in an airtight container, refrigerated, until ready to use.

For the filling: While the pastry is chilling, heat 1 tablespoon of the olive oil and the butter in a skillet over medium heat and add the onions. Season with salt and pepper, reduce the heat to low, and cook and stir for 10–15 minutes, until the onions are soft and starting to caramelize. Add the vinegar, 1½ tablespoons of the thyme, and the sugar and continue to cook, stirring often, for 10–15 minutes more, until all the liquid has cooked out and the onions are caramelized.

While the onions are cooking, toss the remaining olive oil with the tomatoes, season with salt and pepper, and place on a rimmed baking sheet in the oven to roast for 25–30 minutes, until the tomatoes start to burst and shrivel up.

When ready to bake, brush the edges of the tart shell with the egg wash and prick the bottom 8–10 times with a fork. Place in the oven to bake for about 15 minutes, until golden brown and puffed up but not fully cooked. Remove from the oven and spread the whipped feta evenly in the bottom of the tart. Place the onions and tomatoes on top of the feta and sprinkle with the remaining thyme. Place back in the oven to bake for 8–10 minutes more, until the pastry is golden brown all over and the bottom is crispy. Slice and serve warm with a mixed green salad.

Not Your Mom's Chicken Pot Pie

My mom's version of this classic American dish could be made only one way: boil the chicken, make a sauce with the chicken broth and add peas, carrots, and mushrooms, top with biscuits, and bake until golden brown and bubbly. The early recipe for "Chicken Pie" in Amelia Simmons's American Cookery *of 1796 was made by baking whole pieces of chicken under the crust. Countless versions of the pot pie have appeared over the years— some using shrimp, lobster, beef, lamb, or vegetables only. For me, this dish is cool weather and fall nights when you want to make use of fall squash, greens, and mushrooms. If available, different types of mushrooms such as oyster, chanterelle, or hen of the woods add variety and great flavor.*

MAKES 6–8 SERVINGS

½ recipe Pâte Brisée Piecrust (page 132) or Spelt Pie Crust
   (page 140)
1 (4–4½-pound) whole chicken
1 leek
2 celery stalks
2 bay leaves
Kosher salt and freshly ground black pepper, to taste
1 medium butternut squash, peeled, seeded, and
   cut into ½-inch cubes
2 tablespoons olive oil, divided
6 tablespoons (¾ stick) unsalted butter, divided
4 ounces mixed mushrooms, cleaned and thinly sliced
¼ cup all-purpose flour
1 tablespoon chopped fresh marjoram
1 teaspoon chopped fresh thyme leaves
4 cups reduced chicken broth the chicken was cooked in
3 handfuls baby spinach
Egg wash made with 1 egg whisked with 1 tablespoon milk

Preheat the oven to 400°. Butter a 9 × 13-inch ovenproof dish, place on a rimmed baking sheet, and set aside.

Place the chicken in a large stockpot and fill with enough cold water to cover the chicken by about 1 inch. Wash and trim the leek and celery, adding the trimmings to the stockpot. Thinly slice the white and light green parts of the leek and set aside. Thinly slice the celery and set aside. Add the bay leaves to the stockpot and season with salt and pepper. Bring to a boil, reduce the heat to medium low, and simmer the chicken for 50–55 minutes, until the juices run clear when the thigh is pierced with the tip of a small knife.

While the chicken is cooking, toss the squash with 1 tablespoon of the olive oil and 1 tablespoon of the butter, season with salt and pepper, and spread evenly on a rimmed baking sheet. Place in the oven to bake until tender and golden brown, about 30 minutes. Remove from the oven and place in a large bowl to cool slightly. Using the same pan, toss the mushrooms with the remaining olive oil and place in the oven to roast for 10–15 minutes until golden brown. Remove from the oven and add to the bowl with the squash. Reduce the oven temperature to 375°.

When the chicken is done, remove it from the pot and set aside until cool enough to handle. Raise the heat to high to reduce the broth by half. Pick the meat from the chicken and add it to the bowl with the squash, discarding the skin and bones.

In a large skillet, melt the remaining butter over medium heat and cook the sliced leeks and celery for about 2 minutes, until soft but not brown. Add the flour, marjoram, and thyme and cook, stirring constantly, about 2 minutes longer. Slowly whisk in the broth and bring to a low boil, stirring constantly until slightly thick, 2–3 minutes.

Add the chicken, squash, mushrooms, and spinach to the skillet, season with salt and pepper, and stir to mix. Reduce the heat and simmer, stirring occasionally, just until the spinach wilts, 2–3 minutes. Remove from the heat, pour into the prepared dish, and cool slightly.

On a lightly floured surface, roll the pastry and cut it into a shape to fit the top of the baking dish with a slight overlap. Chill the pastry in the refrigerator while the filling cools. When ready to bake, lay the pastry over the top of the dish, allowing the excess to drape about ½ inch over the sides. Tuck the edges under to seal and crimp or press with a fork. Brush with the egg wash and cut several slits in the top; decorate with the trimmings if desired. Place in the oven to bake for 30–35 minutes, until the pastry is golden brown and the filling is bubbling around the edges. Remove from the oven and cool about 10 minutes before serving. Serve warm, making sure to scoop a piece of pastry with each serving.

Creamy Chicken Turnovers

When Craig Claiborne was a young boy, his mother ran a boardinghouse in Indianola, Mississippi. With the tables set with linen, silver, and fine china, the boardinghouse soon became a meeting place for locals as well as travelers. His mother was an excellent self-taught cook, visiting New Orleans often and coming home to re-create the dishes she was served in restaurants there. This recipe is an adaptation of Craig's mother's recipe for chicken turnovers, with the addition of spinach and wrapped in buttery Rough Puff Pastry. I think this recipe would make Craig happy.

MAKES 8 TURNOVERS / SERVES 6–8

---

1 recipe Rough Puff Pastry (page 136)

1 tablespoon olive oil, divided

1 bunch spinach, stems removed, roughly chopped

2 tablespoons (¼ stick) unsalted butter

1 leek, trimmed and diced

2 tablespoons all-purpose flour

1 cup milk

½ cup heavy cream

2 large egg yolks, lightly beaten

Kosher salt and freshly ground black pepper, to taste

2 teaspoons hot sauce

1 teaspoon Worcestershire sauce

¼ teaspoon freshly grated nutmeg

2 cups chopped cooked chicken

Egg wash made with 1 egg whisked with 1 tablespoon milk

In a large skillet, heat 1 teaspoon of the olive oil over medium heat until hot. Add the spinach and sauté until wilted. Remove from the heat and drain well.

In the same skillet, heat the remaining olive oil and butter over medium heat until melted. Add the leeks and cook, stirring, until wilted, about 2 minutes. Add the flour and cook for about 2 minutes more, stirring constantly to avoid browning the flour. Slowly whisk in the milk and cream, whisking constantly until thick. Remove from the heat and whisk in the yolks. Season with salt, pepper, hot sauce, Worcestershire, and nutmeg and stir to combine. Stir in the chicken and set aside to cool slightly.

Remove the dough from the refrigerator and divide in half. On a lightly floured surface, roll each half into a 10 × 10-inch square about ⅛ inch thick. Cut each square into 4 pieces, about 5 × 5 inches each. Chill 4 of squares in the refrigerator. Place the other 4 squares on a rimmed baking sheet lined with parchment paper or lightly greased. Brush the outer edges of each with the egg wash. Spoon equal portions (about 2 heaping tablespoons) of the filling into the center of each pastry, not going all the way to the edges, and fold the dough over into triangles to enclose the filling. Press around the edges of the pastry with a fork or your fingers to seal. Chill in the refrigerator for about 30 minutes. Repeat the process with the remaining pastry and filling.

When ready to bake, preheat the oven to 400°.

Brush the tops of the pastry with the egg wash and prick with a fork to make air vents. Place the turnovers on the center rack in the oven to bake for 22–25 minutes, rotating the pan halfway through, until golden brown and puffed. Serve warm with a tossed green salad.

Carolina Crab Pie

Made with blue crab meat from the coast of North Carolina, South Carolina, or Virginia, this classic savory pie can't be beat. Think crab dip in a pastry, it is so moist and rich; all you need to wash it down is an ice-cold beer.

MAKES ONE 9-INCH PIE / SERVES 6–8

One 9-inch parbaked (pages 16–17) Pâte Brisée Piecrust
    (page 132) or Everyday Flaky Piecrust (page 130)
¼ cup panko bread crumbs, divided
2 large eggs, lightly beaten
½ cup mayonnaise
½ cup milk
1 tablespoon all-purpose flour
1 cup grated sharp cheddar cheese
1 cup grated Swiss or Gruyère cheese
⅓ cup grated onion
¼ cup thinly sliced fresh basil, plus more for garnish
1 tablespoon Dijon mustard
2 teaspoons hot sauce
1 teaspoon Old Bay Seasoning
½ teaspoon kosher salt
¼ teaspoon freshly ground black pepper
½ pound lump crabmeat

Preheat the oven to 350°.

Place the prepared crust on a rimmed baking sheet and sprinkle the bottom with 2 tablespoons of the bread crumbs.

In a large bowl, whisk together the eggs, mayonnaise, milk, and flour until blended. Add the cheddar, Swiss or Gruyère, onions, basil, mustard, hot sauce, Old Bay, salt, and pepper and stir to mix. Pick through the crab, removing any small bits of shell and leaving the meat in large chunks. Gently stir the crab into the cheese mixture, trying not to break it up as you stir.

Pour the mixture into the prepared crust and sprinkle with the remaining bread crumbs. Place on the center rack in the oven to bake for 40–45 minutes, rotating halfway through, until the pastry is golden brown and the pie is set and slightly puffy. Remove from the oven and cool to room temperature, about 30 minutes, before slicing. Serve warm or at room temperature.

Natchitoches Meat Pies

Pronounced NACK-a-tish, Natchitoches is a town in northern Louisiana made famous by this spicy meat pie and the movie Steel Magnolias. *Filled with ground beef and pork, similar to an empanada, this pastry is popular throughout Louisiana. Unlike the customary deep-fried pie, my version is baked. For a more traditional version, try making it with fried pie dough (pages 88–89).*

MAKES EIGHT TO TEN 6-INCH HAND PIES

1 recipe Hand Pie Crust (page 142)
1 tablespoon olive oil
½ pound ground beef
½ pound ground pork
1 small onion, chopped
1 poblano pepper, cored, seeded, and chopped
1 jalapeño pepper, cored, seeded, and chopped
1 tablespoon Old Bay Seasoning
½ teaspoon kosher salt
½ teaspoon freshly ground black pepper
½ teaspoon crushed red pepper flakes
2 tablespoons Worcestershire sauce
1 tablespoon ketchup
1 tablespoon Dijon mustard
1 tablespoon all-purpose flour
1 cup chicken broth
2 tablespoons chopped fresh thyme
Egg wash made with 1 egg lightly whisked with
    1 tablespoon milk

Remove the dough from the refrigerator and divide each piece into 4 equal pieces. On a lightly floured surface, roll each into a 7-inch circle about ⅛ inch thick. Trim the edges to make a 6-inch circle. Reroll the trimmings to make 1 or 2 more 6-inch rounds. Chill in the refrigerator while making the filling.

Heat a large skillet over medium-high heat, add the olive oil, and heat until sizzling. Add the beef and pork, breaking the meat up with a spoon as you add it; cook and stir for about 5 minutes until lightly browned. Add the onions, poblanos, jalapeños, Old Bay, salt, black pepper, and crushed red pepper and cook and stir about 5 minutes more until the vegetables are tender.

Add the Worcestershire, ketchup, mustard, and flour and cook and stir for about 2 minutes. Slowly stir in the broth and bring to a simmer, stirring often. Reduce the heat and simmer for about 5 minutes until slightly thick. Remove from the heat and place in a bowl in the refrigerator to chill.

When ready to bake, preheat the oven to 375°.

Remove the rounds from the refrigerator and place on 1 or 2 rimmed baking sheets lined with parchment paper or lightly greased. Place about 2 heaping tablespoons of the filling on the right side of each round, leaving a ½-inch border.

Brush the edges of the rounds with the egg wash and fold the left side of the dough over the filling so that the edges meet and enclose the filling. Crimp the edges with a fork or your fingers to seal. Cut small vents into the top of each hand pie with a paring knife or prick with a fork.

Brush the tops with the remaining egg wash and sprinkle with salt. Place in the oven on the center rack to bake for 20–25 minutes, rotating halfway through, until golden brown and the filling is bubbling through the vents in the top. Remove from the oven and cool slightly before serving warm.

Oyster Pie with Crispy Saltines

Oyster pie varies from region to region and has long been in south-ern kitchens along the shores from Charleston to New Orleans. Once the poor man's dinner and later served at elegant dinner parties, this dish has been the center of many gatherings. The trick is to keep the oysters tender and the topping crispy. A saltine crust is the perfect fix because this pie can be in the oven for a short time before getting golden brown, making for a perfectly cooked oyster. This dish also makes a great appetizer or hors d'oeuvre.

SERVES 8–10

---

4 tablespoons (½ stick) unsalted butter, divided
1 sleeve saltine crackers, divided
1 tablespoon olive oil
2 ounces diced country ham
1 small onion, diced
2 celery stalks, diced
Kosher salt and freshly ground black pepper, to taste
2 garlic cloves, minced
¼ cup all-purpose flour
2 cups milk
3 handfuls baby spinach leaves, stems removed
¼ cup dry sherry
¼ cup finely chopped parsley
2 teaspoons hot sauce
1 pint shucked oysters, drained, with liquid reserved
2 tablespoons (¼ stick) unsalted butter, melted
   (for brushing the tops of the saltines)

Preheat the oven to 400°. Generously grease a 2-quart oven-safe dish with 1 tablespoon of the butter. Crumble half the sleeve of saltines in the bottom of the dish and set aside.

In a large skillet, heat the olive oil and 1 tablespoon of the butter over medium heat until sizzling hot. Add the ham and cook and stir until crispy, 2–3 minutes. Remove the ham from the skillet and place on a paper towel to drain. Add the onions and celery to the same skillet, season with salt and pepper, cook and stir for 2–3 minutes until the vegetables are tender. Add the garlic and continue to cook and stir for 1 minute more. Add the remaining butter to melt. Add the flour and cook and stir for about 2 minutes longer until the flour is cooked with a little color but not brown. Slowly add the milk, whisking constantly, until the sauce comes to a low boil and starts to thicken, 2–3 minutes. Stir in the spinach, sherry, parsley, and hot sauce and cook just until the spinach wilts. Remove from the heat and stir in the oysters and ¼ cup of their liquid. Taste for seasoning and season with additional salt and pepper if needed.

Brush the top of the crumbled crackers lightly with a portion of the melted butter. Place the dish in the oven to lightly brown and crisp, about 10 minutes. Remove from the oven and pour the filling over the cracker crumbs. Place the remaining saltines (not crumbled) on top. Brush the tops of the crackers with the remaining melted butter and place in the oven to bake until the crackers are golden brown and the filling is bubbling around the edges, about 15 minutes. Remove from the oven and serve hot with a simple tossed salad and a glass of champagne.

Quiche Loretta

I named this quiche Loretta because Julia Child says that a "traditional quiche Lorraine" is simply eggs, cream, and bacon, with a little bit of butter, of course. Her excellent serving suggestions of a dry white wine and a salad or fresh asparagus always work well with this dish. I add cheese, onions, and a few herbs just to give it a little something extra. I think you'll find that you like this combination as well.

MAKES ONE 9-INCH QUICHE / SERVES 6–8

One 9-inch parbaked (pages 16–17) Pâte Brisée Piecrust
    (page 132) or Spelt Piecrust (page 140)
1 tablespoon olive oil
1 tablespoon unsalted butter
1 small onion, diced
3 slices crispy cooked bacon, crumbled
1 cup shredded Gruyère cheese
6 large eggs
1 cup heavy cream
1 teaspoon ground mustard
½ teaspoon kosher salt
¼ teaspoon freshly ground black pepper
Pinch of ground cayenne pepper
¼ teaspoon freshly grated nutmeg

Preheat oven to 350°. Place the prepared piecrust on a rimmed baking sheet and set aside.

In a large skillet, heat the olive oil and butter over medium heat until sizzling. Add the onions and cook and stir for 2–3 minutes until soft and translucent. Remove from the heat and set aside to cool. Sprinkle the onions, bacon, and Gruyère evenly over the bottom of the prepared crust.

In a large bowl, whisk together the eggs, cream, mustard, salt, black pepper, cayenne pepper, and nutmeg until blended. Pour the egg mixture over the cheese mixture in the crust.

Place on the center rack in the oven to bake for 30–35 minutes, rotating halfway through, until the filling is golden and the egg is set around the edges and slightly loose in the center. Remove from the oven and cool about 30 minutes before slicing into wedges. Serve warm or at room temperature with a green salad and a glass of white wine.

Piecrusts

As almost anyone will tell you, the secret to a good pie is in the crust—it should be light, flaky, and delicately crisp. Looking through my grandmother's notebook of recipes, I find so many recipes for piecrusts: "Never Fail Piecrust," "Hot Water Piecrust," "Digestible Crisco Pastry Shell," "Mrs. Edwards' Piecrust," "Fried Piecrust," and more. Everyone has an idea of the perfect crust and how to make it. I even had someone tell me about a piecrust made with a scoop of ice cream instead of butter or shortening, and I'm sure it was delicious. The point is, there are many ways to go about it. Piecrusts have a reputation for being difficult to make, but—and here's the secret—all it takes is a little practice and experience. Give it a few tries, and in no time you will be turning out tender, flaky crusts. See the tips for making piecrusts on pages 12–18.

Let me also pass along some deep wisdom from the *Picayune Creole Cook Book*: "If any pie crust is left, do not think of throwing it away. Take all the bits left from cutting around the edges of the pie pans; roll very thin into small squares; bake lightly and save for tea or luncheon. Put a spoonful of orange, pineapple, lemon or raspberry jelly on each square, and they will be found delicious." My grandmother practiced this. When we made pies together, I always saw her take the trimmings from the crust, sprinkle them with sugar and cinnamon, twirl them into twists or flatten them into rounds, and serve them topped with mashed strawberries. I feel confident about saying the same about almost any pie you spend the time to make: even if you think it is not perfect, "it will be found delicious."

Everyday Flaky Piecrust

My sister Judy gave me this recipe years ago; it's the perfect recipe for a good, flaky piecrust that's easy to work with. She makes her crust with all-vegetable shortening, which makes it extra flaky. I make mine with a mixture of butter and vegetable shortening because I like the flavor of butter as well as the flaky texture the shortening gives the crust.

MAKES TWO 9-INCH PIECRUSTS OR
ONE 9-INCH DOUBLE-CRUST PIE

---

3 cups all-purpose flour, plus more for dusting your
   hands and work surface

3 tablespoons granulated sugar

½ teaspoon kosher salt

½ cup plus 3 tablespoons vegetable shortening,
   cut into small pieces and chilled

8 tablespoons (1 stick) unsalted butter, cut into
   small pieces and chilled

⅓ cup ice water, plus 2–4 more tablespoons as needed

1 large egg

1 tablespoon distilled white vinegar

In a large bowl, stir together the flour, sugar, and salt. Add the shortening and butter and cut it into the flour mixture with a handheld pastry blender or your fingertips until the mixture resembles coarse meal with pea- to almond-size pieces of butter and a few larger chunks. It is important to work quickly to make this dough so that the butter and shortening remain cold.

In a separate small bowl, beat the egg with ⅓ cup of the water and the vinegar. Pour the egg around the edges of the flour mixture while working it into the mixture with a fork just until the dough starts to clump together. Do not over mix. If the dough is too dry, add more water, 1 tablespoon at a time, until the dough comes together.

Lightly dust your hands and work surface with flour. Turn the dough out onto the surface and press it together. Divide the dough in half and shape each piece into a flat, round disk. Cover with plastic wrap and refrigerate for at least 30 minutes or up to 3 days.

Remove the chilled dough from the refrigerator and place it on a lightly floured surface. If the dough is too hard, let it sit for 5–10 minutes before rolling. Dust a rolling pin with flour and roll the dough to form a 12-inch circle about ⅛ inch thick. Brush off any excess flour after rolling. Fold the dough in half or gently roll it up onto the rolling pin and lift to place in a 9-inch pie pan. Press the dough lightly into the bottom and up the sides of the pan.

Trim the edges of the dough with a pair of kitchen shears, leaving about ½ inch of dough draping over the side. Turn the extra dough under itself. Crimp the edge of the pie or flatten it with the tines of a fork. Cover with plastic wrap and refrigerate or freeze for at least 1 hour before baking. Repeat with the other piece of dough. At this point the crust can be wrapped and frozen for up to 2 months. This way you'll always have a piecrust on hand.

To prepare the crust for a double-crust pie, see pages 14–15.

Pâte Brisée Piecrust

Leave it to the French to come up with something so delicious, rich, and buttery. This classic pastry works well for both sweet and savory pies and tarts. I like to pair it with fillings that are tart, such as rhubarb, lemon, or dark chocolate. Try it the next time you make a chicken potpie or quiche; the flavor of this crust enhances any filling.

MAKES TWO 9-INCH PIECRUSTS OR
ONE 9-INCH DOUBLE-CRUST PIE

2½ cups all-purpose flour, plus more for dusting
   your hands and work surface
1 tablespoon granulated sugar
1 teaspoon kosher salt
½ pound (2 sticks) cold unsalted butter,
   cut into small pieces
⅓–½ cup ice water

In a large bowl, stir together the flour, sugar, and salt. Add the butter and cut it into the flour mixture with a handheld pastry blender or your fingertips until the mixture resembles coarse meal with pea- to almond-size pieces of butter and a few larger chunks. It is important to work quickly to make this dough so that the butter and shortening remain cold.

Pour ⅓ cup of the water around the outside edges of the flour mixture and blend with a fork until the dough starts to come together. Do not over mix. If the dough is too dry, add more water, 1 tablespoon at a time, until the dough comes together.

Lightly dust your hands and work surface with flour. Turn the dough out onto the surface and press it together. Divide the dough in half and shape each piece into a flat, round disk. Cover in plastic wrap and refrigerate for at least 30 minutes or up to 3 days.

Remove the chilled dough from the refrigerator and place it on a lightly floured surface. If the dough is too hard, let it sit for 5–10 minutes before rolling. Dust a rolling pin with flour and roll the dough to form a 12-inch circle about ⅛ inch thick. Brush off any excess flour after rolling. Fold the dough in half or gently roll it up onto the rolling pin and lift to place in a 9-inch pie pan. Press the dough lightly into the bottom and up the sides of the pan.

Trim the edges of the dough with a pair of kitchen shears, leaving about ½ inch of dough draping over the side. Turn the extra dough under itself. Crimp the edge of the pie or flatten it with the tines of a fork. Cover with plastic wrap and refrigerate or freeze for at least 1 hour before baking. Repeat with the other piece of dough. At this point the crust can be wrapped and frozen for up to 2 months.

Sweet Tart Crust

This pastry has a crumbly and sandy texture, similar to a butter cookie. It is perfect for tarts because it holds up well on its own. I make this in a tart pan with a removable bottom, and it comes out of the pan perfectly every time. This dough is very forgiving; if it breaks or cracks, simply press it back together. It can be made up to 3 days in advance and refrigerated until ready to use or rolled and put in the pan and frozen up to several months before using. The weather will affect the amount of water you need. When I make this in the winter and the air is dry, I use almost twice as much water as in the summer, when the air is humid.

MAKES TWO 9- OR 10-INCH TART SHELLS

2½ cups all-purpose flour, plus more for dusting
    your hands and work surface
½ cup confectioners' sugar
½ teaspoon kosher salt
12 tablespoons (1½ sticks) cold unsalted butter,
    cut into small pieces
2 large egg yolks
1 teaspoon pure vanilla extract
2–6 tablespoons ice water, as needed

In a large bowl, stir together the flour, sugar, and salt. Cut the butter into the flour mixture using your fingertips or a handheld pastry blender until the butter is blended into the flour mixture and looks like coarse meal with pea- to almond-size pieces of butter and a few larger chunks.

In a separate small bowl, whisk together the egg yolks, vanilla, and 2 tablespoons of the water.

Pour the egg mixture around the outside edges of the flour mixture while blending it with a fork until the dough begins to come together. Do not over mix. If the dough seems dry, add more water, 1 tablespoon at a time, as needed.

Turn the dough onto a lightly floured surface and with floured hands gently press the dough until it comes together in a ball. Divide the dough in half and shape each piece into a flat, round disk. Cover with plastic wrap and refrigerate for at least 30 minutes or up to 3 days.

Remove the chilled dough from the refrigerator and place it on a lightly floured surface. If the dough is too hard, let it sit for 5–10 minutes before rolling. Dust a rolling pin with flour and roll the dough into a 12-inch circle about ⅛ inch thick. Brush off any excess flour after rolling. Press each half into the bottom and up the sides of the tart pan. Press down on the rim of the pan to trim any excess dough. Repeat with the other piece of dough. Cover with plastic wrap and refrigerate for at least 1 hour. At this point the crust can be wrapped and frozen for up to 2 months.

Rough Puff Pastry

This is a recipe I have been making since the early 1980s when I made cheese straws by the thousands for Martha Stewart's catering company in Connecticut. It is an adaptation from Judith Olney's book Summer Food. *I love her no-nonsense approach to recipes, as if she is talking to you while going through the process. I had the pleasure of meeting Judith when I first moved to Durham; she was one of my first customers at Foster's Market. This dough is so easy to work with. I find it easier to do the turns in the next few hours after you make the dough rather than letting it sit overnight, if time will allow. Judith calls for "2 heaped to over-flowing cups of unbleached flour." For me, this is about 2½ cups and works well. This pastry is so flavorful: you can roll out a small amount, top it with thinly sliced apples sprinkled with salt and pepper, and bake until the pastry is crispy—so simple and yet so delicious. Don't throw away those trimmings. Roll them in grated Parmesan cheese and turn them into cheese twists.*

MAKES TWO 9- OR 10-INCH TART SHELLS

2½ cups all-purpose flour, plus more for dusting
   your hands and work surface
½ teaspoon kosher salt
½ pound (2 sticks) cold unsalted butter,
   cut into small pieces
½–¾ cup ice water

In a large bowl, stir together the flour and salt. Add the butter and work into the flour with the tips of your fingers or a hand-held pastry blender until the butter has become almond-sized slicks. Work quickly and stop short rather than overworking.

Pour ½ cup of the water around the outside edges of the dough while blending quickly with a fork to combine, until the dough starts to form a ball. *Judith's advice*: "You will probably use between ⅔ and ¾ cup of water, but instinct should guide rather than a set amount. It is better to err on the side of slightly too much water, as it is easier to work flour into damp pastry rather than water into a tightly bound dough."

Knead the dough 2–3 times to come together, form into a rectangle, cover in plastic wrap, and refrigerate for at least 1 hour or overnight.

Remove the chilled dough from the refrigerator and place it on a lightly floured surface. If the dough is too hard, let it sit for 5–10 minutes before rolling. Roll the dough into a long rectangle. *Judith's advice*: "No larger than it needs to be to fold it into thirds, since over-rolling simply stretches and toughens the dough." Brush off any excess flour after rolling. Fold the dough into thirds, known as a "turn." Roll out again and give it another turn. Wrap and refrigerate for at least 30 minutes. Repeat the process 2 more times (giving it 2 turns each time), for a total of 6 turns. Wrap and refrigerate for at least 1 hour or overnight before rolling as directed in the recipe. See Caramalized Vidalia Onions and Roasted Tomato Tart with Whipped Feta (page 112) and Creamy Chicken Turnovers (page 118).

Cornmeal Cream Cheese Piecrust

We southerners have to get our cornmeal in anywhere we can, not to mention the cream cheese. This is a take on the cream cheese pastry we have all come to know and love and is very easy to work with. I use this for hand pies and empanadas, and it also goes well with lemon and other sweet and savory fillings. Let the dough sit on the counter to warm up a little longer than you would most other pie dough before you begin to roll: it will make it easier to work with.

MAKES TWO 9-INCH PIECRUSTS

- 1½ cups all-purpose flour, plus more for dusting your hands and work surface
- 1 cup yellow cornmeal
- ¼ cup granulated sugar
- ½ teaspoon kosher salt
- ½ teaspoon freshly grated nutmeg
- Finely grated zest of 1 lemon
- 12 tablespoons (1½ sticks) cold unsalted butter, cut into small pieces
- 4 ounces cold cream cheese, cut into small pieces
- 5–8 tablespoons ice water

In a large bowl, stir together the flour, cornmeal, sugar, salt, nutmeg, and lemon zest. Add the butter and cream cheese and blend with a handheld pastry blender or your fingertips until combined and the mixture has a crumbly texture with pea- to almond-size pieces of butter and a few larger chunks.

Add 4 tablespoons of the water around the outside edges of the flour mixture and blend with a fork until the dough comes together and sticks to the side of the bowl. Add more water, 1 tablespoon at a time, as needed until the dough sticks together and starts to form a ball.

Dump the dough onto a piece of plastic wrap or wax paper, divide it in half, and shape each piece into a flat, round disk. Cover with plastic wrap and refrigerate for at least 30 minutes or up to 3 days.

Remove the chilled dough from the refrigerator and place it on a lightly floured surface. If the dough is too hard, let it sit for 5–10 minutes before rolling. Dust a rolling pin with flour and roll the dough to form a 12-inch circle about ⅛ inch thick. Dust off any excess flour. Fold the dough in half or gently roll it up onto the rolling pin and lift to put in a 9-inch pie pan. Press the dough lightly into the bottom and up the sides of the pan.

Trim the edges of the dough with a pair of kitchen shears, leaving about ½ inch of dough draping over the side. Turn the extra dough under itself. Crimp the edge of the pie or flatten it with the tines of a fork. Cover with plastic wrap and refrigerate or place in the freezer at least 1 hour before baking. Repeat with the other piece of dough. At this point the crust can be frozen for up to 2 months. This way you'll always have a piecrust on hand.

Spelt Piecrust

This ancient grain's rich, nutty flavor enhances this pastry to go well with either a hearty filling like Not Your Mom's Chicken Pot Pie (page 115) or a sweet filling like Old-Fashioned Pecan Pie (page 34). This recipe works well with other flours. Try using rye, whole-wheat, or buckwheat flour in place of the spelt.

MAKES TWO 9-INCH PIECRUST OR
ONE 9-INCH DOUBLE-CRUST PIE

1½ cups all-purpose flour, plus more for dusting
    your hands and work surface
1 cup spelt flour
3 tablespoons granulated sugar
½ teaspoon kosher salt
8 tablespoons (1 stick) cold unsalted butter,
    cut into small pieces
⅓ cup (6 tablespoons) vegetable shortening
⅓ cup ice water, plus 2–4 more tablespoons as needed
1 tablespoon apple cider vinegar

In a large bowl, stir together the all-purpose flour, spelt flour, sugar, and salt. Cut the butter and shortening into the flour mixture with a handheld pastry blender or your fingertips until the mixture resembles coarse meal with pea- to almond-size pieces of butter and a few larger chunks. Do this quickly so that the butter remains cold.

Add the vinegar to ⅓ cup of the water and pour around the edges of the flour mixture while blending it with a fork until the dough begins to come together. If it is too dry, add more water, 1 tablespoon at a time, as needed until it clumps together.

Lightly dust your hands and the work surface with flour. Turn the dough out onto the surface and press together. Divide the dough in half and shape each piece into a flat, round disk. Cover in plastic wrap and refrigerate at least 30 minutes or up to 3 days.

Remove the chilled dough from the refrigerator and place it on a lightly floured surface. If the dough is too hard, let it sit for 5–10 minutes before rolling. Dust a rolling pin with flour and roll the dough to form a 12-inch circle about ⅛ inch thick. Dust off any excess flour. Fold the dough in half or gently roll it up onto the rolling pin and lift to put in a 9-inch pie pan. Press the dough lightly into the bottom and up the sides of the pan.

Trim the edges of the dough with a pair of kitchen shears, leaving about ½ inch of dough draping over the side. Turn the extra dough under itself. Crimp the edge of the pie or flatten it with the tines of a fork. Cover with plastic wrap and refrigerate or place in the freezer at least 1 hour before baking. Repeat with the other piece of dough. At this point the crust can be frozen for up to 2 months. This way you'll always have a piecrust on hand.

Hand Pie Crust

I love the idea of individual desserts. It makes everything so easy and your guests feel special: they each get their own little pie. This dough is sturdy enough to use for crostatas and galettes, large and small. Give it a try. It works well with Granny Foster's Fried Apple Pies (page 87); as a nonfried alternative, pop them in the oven to bake.

MAKES EIGHT 6-INCH HAND PIES

2½ cups all-purpose flour, plus more for dusting
   your hands and work surface

3 tablespoons granulated sugar

½ teaspoon kosher salt

½ pound (2 sticks) cold unsalted butter,
   cut into small pieces

1 large egg yolk

4–8 tablespoons ice water

In a large bowl, stir together the flour, sugar, and salt. Cut the butter into the flour mixture using a handheld pastry blender or your fingertips until the butter is blended into the flour mixture and looks like coarse meal with pea- to almond-size pieces of butter and a few larger chunks.

In a separate small bowl, whisk the egg yolk with 4 tablespoons of the water. Pour the egg mixture around the edges of the flour mixture while blending with a fork until the dough begins to come together. Add more water as needed, 1 tablespoon at a time. Do not over mix.

Turn the dough onto a lightly floured surface and with floured hands gently press until it comes together in a ball. Divide the dough in half. For individual pies or crostatas, roll into 2 logs. For larger pies or crostatas, shape into 2 flat, round disks. Cover with plastic wrap and refrigerate at least 1 hour or until ready to use, up to 3 days.

Remove the chilled dough from the refrigerator and place it on a lightly floured surface. If the dough is too hard, let it sit for 5–10 minutes before rolling. For individual pies, divide each log into 4 equal pieces. On a lightly floured surface, roll each piece into a 7-inch circle about ⅛ inch thick. Dust off any excess flour. Trim the edges to make a 6-inch circle. (If you are using this dough for individual crostatas, you do not need to trim the edges; it can be more rustic.) Place the circles on a baking sheet, cover with plastic wrap, and refrigerate until ready to use. Proceed with the directions for the recipe.

Cookie and Cracker Crusts

These no-fail, easy to make piecrusts can be filled with many of the icebox and custard pie recipes in this book. And the crust itself can be made with just about any cracker or cookie, homemade or store-bought. It's my go-to option for gluten-free crust: just crush some gluten free cookies in the food processor and proceed with one of these recipes. At the end of testing recipes when I was cleaning out my pantry, I made some of the best crusts, combining leftover crumbs and turning nuts and cookies into crusts. One of my favorite combinations was dark chocolate–covered almonds, chocolate-covered pretzels, and Oreos. To experiment, all you need to do is add a little more or less butter and sugar, by the tablespoon, here and there. If the cookie is really sweet and buttery, I add a little less butter and sugar; if dry, I add a little more . . . you get the picture. So have fun, clean out that pantry, and let your imagination work here. Below are some of my favorites along with the basics.

Graham Cracker Crust

MAKES ONE 9-INCH PIECRUST

1½ cups graham cracker crumbs (see Notes)
3 tablespoons granulated sugar
¼ teaspoon kosher salt
6 tablespoons (¾ stick) unsalted butter, melted

Preheat the oven to 350°.

In a medium bowl, combine the graham cracker crumbs, sugar, and salt and stir to mix. Add the melted butter and stir until no dry ingredients are visible.

Press the mixture evenly on the bottom and up the sides of a 9-inch pie pan. Freeze or refrigerate until firm, about 30 minutes.

Place on a rimmed baking sheet on the center rack of the oven to bake for 8–10 minutes, just until slightly brown. Remove from the oven and set aside to cool completely before using. The crust will get firm as it cools.

NOTES ❋ To make the cookie crumbs, place broken cookies in a food processor and pulse 8–10 times, then leave the motor running for about 10 seconds, until the crumbs are finely ground.

To form the crust, use a ½-cup measuring cup to press the crumbs into the bottom and up the sides of the pan; it makes a nice, even rim.

VARIATIONS ❋ Reduce the graham cracker crumbs to 1 cup and add ½ cup ground walnuts, pecans, almonds, hazelnuts, peanuts, pretzels, potato chips, or praline. Vanilla wafers also make a great crust; replace the graham cracker crumbs with vanilla wafer crumbs and follow the recipe above.

Black Bottom Crust

1½ cups chocolate wafer cookie crumbs
(or any other chocolate cookie crumbs)
2 tablespoons granulated sugar
Pinch kosher salt
4 tablespoons (½ stick) unsalted butter, melted

Preheat the oven to 350°.

In a medium bowl, stir together the cookie crumbs, sugar, and salt. Pour in the butter and stir to combine until all the crumbs are moist. Press evenly into the bottom and up the sides of a 9-inch pie pan. Freeze or refrigerate until firm, about 30 minutes.

Place on a rimmed baking sheet on the center rack in the oven to bake for 8–10 minutes. Remove from the oven and set aside to cool completely before using. The crust will get firm as it cools.

Gingersnap Crust

1½ cups gingersnap cookie crumbs

2 tablespoons granulated sugar

½ teaspoon kosher salt

4 tablespoons (½ stick) unsalted butter, melted

Preheat the oven to 350°F.

In a medium bowl, stir together the gingersnap crumbs, sugar, and salt. Add the melted butter and stir until moistened.

Press the mixture evenly on the bottom and up the sides of a 9-inch pie pan to form the crust. Freeze or refrigerate until firm, about 30 minutes.

Place on a rimmed baking sheet and place on the center rack in the oven to bake for 8–10 minutes, just until golden brown. Remove from the oven and set aside to cool completely before using. The crust will get firm as it cools.

Saltine Cracker Crust

1½ cups saltine crackers crumbs, made from about
   1¼ sleeve of crackers (see Note)
3 tablespoons granulated sugar
6 tablespoons (¾ stick) unsalted butter, melted

Preheat the oven to 350°.

In a medium bowl, combine the cracker crumbs and sugar and stir to mix. Add the melted butter and stir until the mixture is moistened.

Press the mixture evenly on the bottom and up the sides of a 9-inch pie pan to form the crust. Freeze or refrigerate for 30 minutes until firm.

Place on a rimmed baking sheet on the center rack in the oven to bake for about 15 minutes, just until golden brown and firm. Remove from the oven and set aside to cool completely before using.

NOTE ✳ When you place the crackers in the food processor to make into crumbs, break them into pieces as you put them in. Pulse to crush, but do not crush into a fine dust—you still want some small pieces of cracker left there.

Acknowledgments

First, I would like to thank the Southern Foodways Alliance and Square Books for bringing Elaine Maisner and me together. Even though we live down the road from each other, we had to travel to Oxford, Mississippi, and bump into each other strolling down the aisle of Square Books to connect for this book. The food world is such a small, inviting world, filled with talented, generous people, and I am fortunate to be a part of it. Elaine is the person who brought this series to light and my editor on this book. It has been a privilege to work with her and everyone at the University of North Carolina Press to become part of the *Savor the South* series. I feel honored to be among a group of such distinguished authors and cooks.

Thanks also to all the willing friends and family who generously contributed by sharing recipes and pies with me not only during this project but also over the years. I have been inspired by so many: my grandmother making chocolate meringue pie for me most every Sunday of my childhood; my sister teaching me how to make cherry cream cheese pie when we were in college and so many more throughout our life; my mother showing me that most anyone can put together a pie in a matter of minutes; and all the bakers at Foster's Market over the years, Gretchen Sedaris, Jenn Evetushick, and Chano Hernandez, always accepting the challenge and bringing new light to an old-time tradition of pie making.

A special thanks to all the staff at University of North Carolina Press for fine tuning, organizing, and tweaking to make this a better book, especially Laura Jones Dooley for her diligent edits and Mary Carley Caviness for her guidance and assistance throughout this project. Thanks to Dino Battista and his team for getting the word out about *Pie.*

And last but not least, thanks to all who helped me taste our way through the testing of recipes for this book, especially Peter, my husband, and Patrick, my nephew, for their discriminating critiques. When they really liked a particular pie, they would always say that it needed to be tested again. To all my friends and neighbors in Lake Placid and Durham who shared pies—too many to list—you know who you are.

Suggested Reading

Ayto, John. *An A–Z of Food and Drink*. Oxford: Oxford University Press, 2002.

Blount, Roy, Jr. *Save Room for Pie: Food Songs and Chewy Ruminations*. New York: Farrar, Straus and Giroux, 2016.

Bullock, Helen. *The Williamsburg Art of Cookery or Accomplished Gentlewoman's Companion*. Williamsburg, Va.: Colonial Williamsburg Foundation, 1938.

Child, Julia, Louisette Bertholle, and Simone Beck. *Mastering the Art of French Cooking, Volume One*. New York: Alfred A. Knopf, 1961.

Claiborne, Craig. *Craig Claiborne's Southern Cooking*. Athens: University of Georgia Press, 2007.

Daley, Regan. *In the Sweet Kitchen: The Definitive Baker's Companion*. New York: Artisan, 2001.

Davidson, Alan. *The Oxford Companion to Food*. 2nd ed. Oxford: Oxford University Press, 2006.

Glenn, Camille. *The Heritage of Southern Cooking*. New York: Workman, 1986.

Grigson, Jane. *Jane Grigson's Fruit Book*. New York: Atheneum, 1982.

Heatter, Maida. *Maida Heatter's New Book of Great Desserts*. New York: Alfred A. Knopf, 1982.

Malgieri, Nick. *Nick Malgieri's Pastry: Foolproof Recipes for the Home Cook*. London: Kyle Books, 2014.

Olney, Judith. *Summer Food*. New York: Atheneum, 1983.

The Original Picayune Creole Cook Book. 11th ed. New Orleans, La.: Times Picayune, 1947.

Puckett, Susan. *A Cook's Tour of Mississippi*. Jackson, Miss.: Hederman Brothers, 1980.

Rutledge, Sarah. *The Carolina Housewife*. Columbia: University of South Carolina Press, 1979.

Shere, Lindsey Remolif. *Chez Panisse Desserts*. New York: Random House, 1985.

Shields, David S. *Southern Provisions: The Creation and Revival of a Cuisine*. Chicago: University of Chicago Press, 2015.

Stewart, Martha. *Martha's American Food: The Celebration of Our Nation's Most Treasured Dishes, from Coast to Coast.* New York: Clarkson Potter, 2012.

———. *Martha Stewart's Baking Handbook.* New York: Clarkson Potter, 2005.

Welty, Eudora. "Kin." *New Yorker*, November 15, 1952.

Williams, Mary E., and Katharine Rolston Fisher. *Elements of the Theory and Practice of Cookery: A Text-Book of Household Science for Use in Schools.* New York: Macmillan, 1909.

Index